Early Praise for *QI Skills for the Early Childhood Classroom*

This book is fantastic! Written in a concrete, actionable way, it serves as a recipe for early educator success, equipping teachers with the tools to help young children master the skills they need to thrive in school and life. As a pediatrician for over 25 years, I sincerely hope that *QI Skills for the Early Childhood Classroom* becomes required reading for every early educator.

JULIE KARDOS, MD—Pediatrician, Two Peds in a Pod

I absolutely LOVE this book and wish I had it when I was teaching my university course on Instructing Young Children. Dr. Jana introduces a brilliantly simple framework—QI Skills—that captures the essential skills for a child's future success. With compelling research, real-world anecdotes, and practical tools, this book empowers educators to integrate these skills seamlessly into their classrooms. A must-read for all early childhood educators!

DEBORAH WEBER, PhD—Global Child Development & Play Expert; Founder, Play Elevated, and former Sr. Director of Early Childhood Development Research, Fisher-Price, Inc.

This book proves that you can be scientific without being stuffy, and practical without being superficial. I've trained educators for years, and Dr. Laura's QI Skill Framework and strategy for cultivating foundationally important human skills hits the sweet spot that all educators deserve.

CHRIS DANILO—Learning facilitator and trainer

Dr. Jana's QI Skills framework is invaluable in shaping early childhood development. Our parents consistently say they want their children to learn fundamentally important life skills, and this book makes it possible. Her writing provides educators with practical strategies to develop these skills and helps us train our faculty to partner effectively with parents in preparing young learners for the future.

RACHEL VAN EMON—Owner, Primrose Schools of Woburn, Burlington and Chelmsford

This book is both timely and essential for early educators who want to create learning environments that truly support young children's healthy development. I love the practical layout, the integration of brain science, and the real-world classroom relevance. Dr. Jana's introduction to the QI Skills framework provides educators with a clear roadmap for meeting children where they are and nurturing their cognitive and social growth.

BEN STEPHENSON—Headteacher, Nanstallon Primary School, Cornwall, UK

Dr. Jana has done it again! *QI Skills for the Early Childhood Classroom* is the playbook educators need to prepare young children for the future. Breaking down QI into seven essential skills, she offers a brilliantly simple yet profoundly effective approach to early education. Every early childhood teacher should have this book in their hands.

NOEL J. RIGLEY, PhD—Owner, 8 Primrose educational childcare centers

There are countless parenting books, but far too few resources specifically for early childhood educators and childcare providers. As a longtime fan of Dr. Jana's work, I was thrilled to see her QI Skills framework applied to the early childhood classroom. This book is exactly what our teachers need—offering practical takeaways, developmental milestones, and reflection activities that fit seamlessly into real-world classrooms. The Classroom QI-nnections section is a game-changer!

ROBERT PATTERSON—CEO, Kids Can Community Center

Grammar Factory Publishing
MacMillan Company Limited
25 Telegram Mews, 39th Floor, Suite 3906
Toronto, Ontario, Canada
M5V 3Z1

www.grammarfactory.com

Jana, Laura A.
QI Skills for the Early Childhood Classroom: A Guide to Nurturing the Human Skills That Matter Most in an AI-Powered World / Laura A. Jana, MD.

Paperback ISBN 978-1-998528-24-0
eBook ISBN 978-1-998528-25-7
Audiobook ISBN 978-1-998528-26-4

1. EDU009000 Education / Educational Psychology.
2. PSY004000 Psychology / Developmental / Child.
3. FAM012000 Family & Relationships / Child Development.

Production Credits
Cover design by Designerbility
Interior layout design by Setareh Ashrafologhalai
Book production and editorial services by Grammar Factory Publishing

Grammar Factory's Carbon Neutral Publishing Commitment
Grammar Factory Publishing is proud to be neutralizing the carbon footprint of all printed copies of its authors' books printed by or ordered directly through Grammar Factory or its affiliated companies through the purchase of Gold Standard-Certified International Offsets.

Disclaimer
The material in this publication is of the nature of general comment only and does not represent professional advice. It is not intended to provide specific guidance for particular circumstances, and it should not be relied on as the basis for any decision to take action or not take action on any matter which it covers. Readers should obtain professional advice where appropriate, before making any such decision. To the maximum extent permitted by law, the author and publisher disclaim all responsibility and liability to any person, arising directly or indirectly from any person taking or not taking action based on the information in this publication.

QI SKILLS

FOR THE EARLY
CHILDHOOD CLASSROOM

QI SKILLS

FOR THE EARLY

CHILDHOOD CLASSROOM

A Guide to Nurturing the Human
Skills That Matter Most in an
AI-Powered World

LAURA A. JANA, MD

GRAMMAR
FACTORY
— EST⁰ 2013 —

CONTENTS

. . . .

INTRODUCTION
Key Skills for the Early Childhood Classroom

. . . .

A S AN early educator, you have a unique opportunity to nurture a key set of skills recognized as playing a significant role in shaping each child's future. That will be the focus of this book. I'll provide practical advice on what you can do to create classroom experiences and interactions that help children assemble their lifelong toolkit of skills. Ultimately, what this means is that you get to play one of the lead roles as brain builder by helping young children make important connections, right down to the level of connecting neurons in their developing brains.

Before we head *inside* the early childhood classroom, however, we're going to take a very brief but highly relevant look at what's going on in the world *outside* of your classroom. This big-picture perspective is meant to make it clear just why these skills are so valuable, why it's so important to focus on strategic skill development so early in children's lives, and, of course, explain in a bit more detail the leading role you stand to play.

Why now?

While a detailed explanation of global trends is far beyond the scope of this book, I've found that to better understand the importance of the skills we will be discussing throughout this book, one only needs to consider three main shifts that are already redefining the world our children will live in. These are:

1   Easier access to far more information than ever before.

2   A world that continues to become increasingly complex and globally connected.

3   Rapid change, in large part fueled by technology.

So, then, the question becomes: *What skills will children need to thrive in this brave new AI-powered world?*

When information is so easily accessed via a quick Google (or ChatGPT) search, it only makes sense that curiosity, critical thinking, and the ability to ask good questions become far more useful than just memorizing and reciting answers. Similarly, when faced with new and previously unknown challenges that inevitably arise during times of rapid change, it is the ability to explore, try new things, persevere, and adapt in the face of failure and setbacks that makes it possible to rise to the challenge much more effectively than simply being a good rule follower.

"We are currently preparing students for jobs and technologies that don't yet exist . . . in order to solve problems we don't even know are problems yet."

RICHARD RILEY
former U.S. Secretary of Education

While mastering the more traditional "hard" skills like reading, writing and arithmetic—which, going forward, we will refer to as "IQ Skills"—remains unquestionably important, this is not enough to succeed in today's world. Increasingly, "soft" skills and abilities such as creativity, communication, collaboration, teamwork, critical thinking, curiosity, initiative, persistence, adaptability, leadership, and social and cultural awareness are being recognized as necessary to excel in classrooms and boardrooms alike.

A DIFFERENT KIND OF
TEACHING AND LEARNING

"For more than two decades, researchers, educators, policy-makers and business leaders have emphasized the need to support '21st-century' skills in a context where knowledge is rapidly expanding, and technologies and work processes are rapidly changing. These abilities include critical thinking and problem-solving skills; the capacity to find, analyze, synthesize and apply knowledge to novel situations; interpersonal skills that allow people to work with others and engage effectively in cross-cultural contexts; self-directional abilities that allow them to manage their own work and complex projects . . . and the capacity to communicate effectively in many ways. Scholars in the learning sciences have emphasized that developing these kinds of skills requires a different kind of teaching and learning than that emphasized in prior eras of education when learning was conceptualized as the acquisition of facts and teaching as the transmission of information to be taken in and used 'as is.'"

LINDA DARLING-HAMMOND ET AL, "Implications for educational practice of the science of learning and development" (2020)

Why (so) early?

Turning our attention to how best to "assemble" this new toolkit of life-enhancing skills, let's start by addressing the question of when is the best time to assemble it. The short answer is: "the earlier the better." While some believe that we should at least let young children learn to stand on their own two feet, toddle out of their diapers, and enjoy a few carefree years of childhood before jumping into formal skill-building, the fact of the matter is that the kind of strategic skill-building we will be discussing allows for just that. With an emphasis on talking, reading, cooing, singing, and playfully engaging with young children, the science of early brain and child development tells us, in no uncertain terms, that these sorts of interactions *are* skill-building activities. It also reinforces the fact that the first five years represent a particularly critical window for foundational learning and skill development.

From skill-building to brain-building

Our early years are defined by incredibly rapid brain growth. From a structural standpoint, an impressive 85% of this complex neural architecture is thought to be constructed within the first three years. Babies are born with 100 billion neurons (a number said to rival the number of stars in the Milky Way!). These brain cells connect at a mind-expanding rate of up to 1 million new neural connections (synapses) per second. With respect to the "wiring" of the brain, it should come as no surprise that the underlying pathways responsible for basic vision and hearing, present at birth, are the first to develop, followed soon thereafter by early language skills later in the first year.

The brain circuitry responsible for what are commonly referred to as "higher" cognitive functions like thinking, reasoning, and communicating, as well as social skills such as patience, delayed gratification, and the ability to manage conflict, are all largely in place by age five.[1] These and other so-called "executive function skills" develop at their most rapid rate between the ages of three and five years.

EFs: AS IMPORTANT AS THE ABCs?

Executive function skills, which are sometimes referred to by researchers in the world of early child development as "EFs," are formally defined as:

1 Impulse control
2 Cognitive flexibility
3 Working memory

Executive function skills are proving to be more strongly associated with school readiness than traditional measures such as IQ, math skills, or even the ABCs of entry-level reading.[2]

While all of this rapid growth and connecting of brain cells in the early years is impressive, it's not simply a matter of he or she with the most connections "wins." Even a mind-blowing number of neural connections doesn't guarantee a child will thrive. In fact, while the number of synapses increases significantly from birth to two years, after that they naturally start to thin out based on whether or not those pathways are being used. Those that are put to good use are strengthened, while those that aren't are pruned away. So the question becomes, how best to strengthen the right connections?

Why you?

This brings us full circle to the final question to be addressed before heading into our classroom-focused discussion: What role do you (and I, and all early educators) play in all of this brain- and skill-building? Again, the short answer is that you have the opportunity to play a starring role. Neurons don't just connect, and young children don't just develop all of the crucial skills they'll need without human connection. Right down to the wiring of babies' brains, unlocking children's early learning potential and strengthening these connections is deeply dependent on engaged, social, back-and-forth, or what are also referred to as "serve-and-return" interactions with caring, responsive adults.

All told, what we now have is an established group of flexible skills broadly recognized as being of the utmost importance for success in today's AI-powered, rapidly changing, and globally complex world. As we've also touched on, we know that the foundational development of these skills happens in early childhood, and that development is best nurtured and strengthened through engaged interactions with caring, responsive adults.

That's why, nearly a decade ago, I set out on a mission to make it easier for everyone—including early educators—to better recognize, understand, remember, embrace, prioritize and nurture these valuable skills. As an important first step, I quickly realized that this meant coming up with a better name for them, so we could more easily describe and effectively apply these skills in our classrooms and our daily lives. Allow me now to introduce you to the QI Skills.

PART 1

QI SKILLS

What's in a Name?

"Shared language serves as the linguistic glue that binds individuals, facilitating a deeper understanding and smoother collaboration."[3]

INSTITUTE FOR SOCIAL CAPITAL

"Because different fields and sectors may not use the same categorizations and vocabulary for [all of the elements that contribute to child development and early learning], developing practices . . . that support more consistent and continuous development and early learning . . . will require a concerted effort to communicate clearly and come to a mutual understanding of the goals for children."[4]

TRANSFORMING THE WORKFORCE
FOR CHILDREN BIRTH THROUGH
AGE 8: A UNIFYING FOUNDATION

THE FIRST TIME I was introduced to the word *qi*, I admit I had to ask what it meant. The answer I got came in the form of a question: "Do you know the phrase, 'May the Force be with you!' from *Star Wars*?" tech and gaming entrepreneur Vishal Gondal asked me over a serendipitous dinner. "*Qi* represents *that* force." Already months into my search for a more fitting name to call all of the "soft," "non-cognitive" and "other" skills that have their foundational development in early childhood, that introduction was more than enough to grab my attention. After all, the collective skills we're talking about have proven themselves to be a powerful force for good in children's and adults' lives. The fact that the word *qi* can be pronounced "key" only serves to make it an even more optimal choice to express just how foundationally important these skills really are.

ALPHABET SOUP AND THE NEED FOR QI

The list of skills now recognized as the ones children will need to succeed has changed considerably from the predominantly academic, cognitive, fact-based abilities of days past. Added to this new priority list of "soft," "non-cognitive" and "other" skills are highly valued traits and abilities like creativity, curiosity, communication, collaboration, and critical thinking. In addition to these all-important "five Cs," a fourth "R" added to the traditional three (phonetic) Rs of reading, writing and (a)rithmetic serves to elevate the importance of relationships. And, of course, added to the mix are empathy, grit, perseverance, and the ability to fail and adapt. At the core of this alphabet-soup-like list of coveted abilities are a host of additional skills variously referred to as character skills, people skills, life skills, emotional intelligence (EI), social-emotional learning (SEL), and executive function skills (EFS).

The problem is that calling all of these all-important skills "soft" really doesn't do them justice in a world where hard skills are still heavily favored. Referring to them as "non-cognitive" is just plain wrong, since these (and all skills, if you stop to think about it) have everything to do with the brain and cognition. That leaves us with "other," and, as someone with more than 20 years of media and communications experience, I can assure you that if ever you want to convince somebody that something is important, it's a really bad idea to settle for calling it "other!" Hence the need for a more fitting word or name to call these key skills. Enter *qi*.

As a concept describing "the flow of energy that sustains human beings," *qi* has been synonymous with life force well before it reached pop-culture fame. Thought to permeate all living things and link elements together, *qi* is believed to be both something we're born with (*yuan qi*) and something we can cultivate, develop and learn—a characteristic that fits with what you'll soon discover is true of each of the seven QI Skills I will introduce you to in the following chapters. While *qi* has commonly been associated with traditional Chinese culture (where it's more often pronounced "chee"), concepts very similar to *qi* have been around for centuries and recognized across cultures—from Hindu, ancient Greek and Hawaiian to Tibetan, Buddhist and Hebrew—all meaning some form of positive or vital life force. For anyone actively searching for a word best suited to describe a set of universal life skills—which I most certainly was—*qi*, as "the life process or flow of energy that sustains living beings," definitely fits the bill.[5]

QI STANDS FOR QUALITY IMPROVEMENT

The pairing of the letters "Q" and "I" actually has a well-established use in health care and other systems, where QI is commonly understood to represent "quality improvement." What all QI approaches have in common is the ultimate goal of supporting and continually improving quality—an additional meaning and application of the letters QI that also fits particularly well for our purposes, given the role that fostering all of the "soft," "non-cognitive" and "other" skills stands to play in continually improving the quality of children's lives.

Finally, as if all of these meanings and uses alone weren't convincing enough, the word *qi*, when used in its capitalized form as QI (which I have intentionally done to clearly distinguish QI Skills as a formal framework from the general concept of *qi*), serves as a perfect complement to the IQ Skills. The traditional three Rs, for example, are still really important; as a longtime literacy advocate, I would never suggest otherwise. But in order for children to truly thrive, they need both skillsets, the complementary nature of which is now conveniently represented by the same letters in reverse order: IQ and QI.

So there you have it. Having found an all-encompassing word that represents a positive life force recognized for centuries and across cultures, a word that conveniently sounds like "key" and serves as a complement to IQ (Skills), and a word that even when mistaken to mean "quality improvement" still describes the opportunity that nurturing and strengthening these skills in your classroom offers during the earliest years of children's lives, allow me to present to you the seven QI Skills. They are:

- ME
- WE
- WHY
- WILL
- WIGGLE
- WOBBLE
- WHAT IF

Should you find these skills, when read aloud, to sound a bit like something out of a Dr. Seuss book, know that that's the intent. While there should be no doubt that the concepts they represent are serious (and, I should add, seriously evidence-based), the QI Skills and their applications—in the classroom and beyond—are meant to be fun. Similarly, QI Skills aim to help you take all that we know about early brain and child development, combine that with what's going on in the world today, and practically apply it in your daily interactions with young children.

What this book is *not* about is memorizing the definitions of yet one more new set of skills. Rather, my hope is that this book will empower you by giving you an intuitive understanding and real gut feel for the QI Skills and how best to bring them to life in your early childhood classroom.

In the spirit of helping you transition to a deeper dive into the QI Skills, here's a general outline of what lies ahead. In each of the following seven chapters I will focus on a single QI Skill—describing it, showing you how to recognize it, and explaining why it's so important for success in today's complex and rapidly changing AI-powered world. As any self-respecting pediatrician would, I'll also offer you a new way of thinking about the developmental milestones of early childhood and relevant ways to view them through a QI Skill lens.

Each chapter will also offer you what I'm calling Classroom "QI-nnections"—a set of fun and practical strategies for the day-to-day application of each individual QI Skill. Rounding out each chapter will be a set of QI Takeaways meant to serve as a quick summary listing of each skill's key points—including ones meant to address or clarify common misunderstandings—along with a QI Reflections section that, by offering you a few thought-provoking questions, will help you think more deeply about how each of the QI Skills applies to you, your students, and your daily classroom curriculum, activities and interactions. As an added bonus, you'll find a set of additional QI-enhancing strategies that apply to all of the QI Skills conveniently pulled together in a Quick Start Guide located at the end of the book.

ME
Focusing Attention on Self-Management

. . . .

"He that controls others may be powerful, but he who has mastered himself is mightier still."

LAO TZU

NSTEAD OF just defining our first QI Skill right out of the gate, I want to start with an example of a ME-related behavior that has a way of making just about everyone uncomfortable: biting. Whether it presents as a seemingly random or isolated incident or it becomes a challenging habit, biting has two key aspects that apply to just about every instance in which it occurs:

1 Biting tends to be more than a little frustrating for everyone involved—from parents, to teachers, to those being bitten and, yes, even for the child doing the biting. This has a way of making biting incidents even more stressful and emotionally charged.

2 The fact that young children bite is, in a great many instances, developmentally normal.

That's right—as challenging as this toothy problem can be, it is equally important to acknowledge that the underlying impulse that drives young children to commit such a classroom-disturbing act is, in fact, normal. The reason why biting seems to rise above all other impulsive behaviors of early childhood in its ability to cause distress is not because it is inherently any more developmentally concerning (it's not). Rather, biting just happens to be the least socially acceptable of all of the predictable, impulse-driven behaviors of early childhood.

What's biting got to do with ME?

If you stop and think about it, so many of the things we routinely expect young children to do and not do—keeping their hands to themselves, sitting still, waiting their turns, and not hitting, throwing things at or, of course, biting their friends—all depend on their ability to employ newly emerging self-control and impulse-control skills.

As skills which involve controlling and regulating one's behaviors, these are tools I have classified as ME Skills. How capable any given child is at applying these fundamentally valuable self-management skills in their day-to-day interactions varies considerably depending on a whole host of factors, including everything from their surroundings in the classroom (or at home) to their age, personality, how tired they are, or their present mood.

> ✋ **ME Skills** are the self-management skills that allow children to be in control of their own thoughts, feelings, and actions. They include self-awareness, self-control, identity, focus, and attention.

ME defined

As the word "me" implies, ME Skills can be thought of as the inward-facing skills that allow all of us to be in better control of our thoughts, feelings and actions, which, in the case of young children, includes biting. While inward-facing at their core, the ME Skills set the stage for all of the more outward-facing, engagement-focused QI Skills to follow. Given the fundamental and foundational importance of these self-management skills, ME Skills are first among the seven QI Skills.

The following concepts, with which you're likely already well familiar, are all included in ME Skills:

- Self-awareness
- Self-control
- Impulse control
- Self-management

- Self-regulation
- Focus
- Attention
- Identity

ME Skills also include such abilities as inner focus, mindfulness, and the self-focused aspects of emotional intelligence related to being in touch with oneself and one's emotions. In fact, ME Skills feature prominently in what is considered by many to be the gold-standard definition of social and emotional learning (SEL) offered by CASEL—the Collaborative for Academic, Social, and Emotional Learning. For those of you not familiar with CASEL, it is a national organization expressly committed to helping make evidence-based social and emotional learning an integral part of education. In alignment with some of the more academic and educational terminology you may have heard or learned about, the relevance of ME Skills is most notable for SEL's definitional focus on "the acquisition and application of knowledge, skills, and attitudes necessary to develop healthy identities, manage emotions, achieve personal goals, and make responsible decisions."[6]

In addition to SEL, also at the heart of ME Skills are the executive function skills we touched upon in the introduction— the brain-based skills that start developing surprisingly early in life and ultimately allow all of us (children and adults alike) to manage, regulate, and control our emotions and behavior, not to mention the underlying and highly prized cognitive processes responsible for reasoning, planning, and problem-solving. These are skills that have proven themselves, for good reason, to be of particular interest and value not just in early childhood but also throughout life. It's worth noting that by 12 months of age, young children's experiences are already laying the foundation for the development of executive function skills—and, as you'll recall, these valuable ME Skills have their most rapid rate of development between the ages of three and five.[7]

While it's thus useful for all early educators to be familiar with and ideally aim to model and cultivate these executive function skills in the early years, it's at least as important to recognize that, in young children, the ME Skills—with executive function skills serving as a core component—take time to develop. As Harvard's Center on the Developing Child sums it up, "No one is born with executive function skills, but nearly everyone can learn them. Our genes provide the blueprint for learning these skills, but they develop through experiences and practice."[8]

Biting serves as a particularly useful example when thinking about what ME Skills and executive functioning look like in young children, if for no other reason than because the ME-defining executive function skills are, for the most part, notably absent in the first few years. The part of the brain responsible for impulsive behaviors, called the amygdala, is dominant in the early years of brain development—that is, until the prefrontal cortex, home to the executive function skills, starts to gain control. It's not that two- or three-year-olds *never* demonstrate any degree of self-control; it's just that stopping and thinking through one's actions rather than simply acting (say, biting) on impulse doesn't realistically happen without the executive-function skill development necessary to do so. In short, expecting too much in the way of polished ME Skills during the early years—especially those involving impulse control—before their established period of rapid development would be as unrealistic as expecting toddlers to tie their own shoelaces.

LENDING YOUNG CHILDREN USE OF OUR EXECUTIVE FUNCTION SKILLS

As a defining feature of ME Skills, executive function skills can admittedly seem somewhat abstract. I was therefore particularly excited to come across neuroscience researcher Bruce Wexler's considerably more practical way of explaining how best to nurture these valuable skills. In his book *Brain and Culture: Neurobiology, Ideology, and Social Change*,[9] Wexler suggests that we can model the use of executive function skills. We can show children how to begin to apply this higher level of thinking and reasoning to their decision-making by demonstrating how we do it ourselves. Think of it like training wheels or a sippy cup: by "lending" young children the use of your executive function skills, you're providing a temporary assist that will allow them, over time, to develop and ultimately rely on their own higher-order thinking to stop, think through, and guide their actions.

The purpose of this chapter is to help you better recognize ME Skills, understand their importance, set realistic expectations, and recognize the many opportunities you have to encourage, model and cultivate them in your daily classroom routines.

Me: NOT the center of the universe

Although the QI Skills are all quite intuitive, the name "ME Skills" can sometimes lead to a misunderstanding. To clear up any confusion, I've found that it's useful at the outset to share not just what ME Skills *are*, but also what they *are not*.

When my son was a toddler, he had a T-shirt featuring a disproportionately large stick figure standing on a very small Earth with planets orbiting around it and a large, bold arrow pointing to the figure. The equally bold caption read, "Me: the center of the universe!" At the time, I thought the T-shirt was both cute and served as a pretty accurate representation of how most two-year-olds see the world. However, picture the same shirt on a 22-year-old (in a larger size, of course) and the same declaration would be significantly less cute and quite a bit more concerning. Given the pervasive worry that many children today are being taught that they are the center of the world and are growing up with a corresponding sense of entitlement, I want to make it clear that this is *not* what's meant by ME Skills. In fact, instead of being hyper-focused on oneself to the detriment of others, ME Skills are all about the self-awareness and self-management that serve to enhance interactions with others.

Why ME?

Since the 1990s, lots of early childhood discussions about self-management have begun with marshmallows. This is thanks to research conducted by Stanford psychologist Walter Mischel starting in the 1960s, now commonly referred to as Mischel's Marshmallow Experiment.[10] Mischel's landmark research sought to better understand the development of self-control and deferred gratification in preschoolers, and whether these early abilities had implications for children's future life outcomes. One by one, each of Mischel's young test subjects was brought into a room where a single marshmallow was placed in front of them. The children were told that if they waited 15 minutes for the researcher to return to the room, they would be rewarded with two marshmallows instead of just the one. If they couldn't wait that long, however, they were told that all they had to do was simply ring the bell and the researcher would promptly return, but they'd only get to eat a single marshmallow. With that, each young child was left alone to face their sweet temptation. Their internal struggles, caught on video, were both adorable and revealing.

The young subjects spanned the self-restraint spectrum. Some succumbed immediately to temptation and simply ate the marshmallow. Others were able to wait long enough to be rewarded with a second marshmallow. Those who managed to resist giving in to temptation did so by exercising any number of clever techniques—some covered their eyes, turned around so they couldn't see it, tugged their hair, or even stroked the marshmallow.

Adding what seemed to be significantly more weight to these marshmallow results was the fact that follow-up studies decades later revealed that the preschoolers who waited the longest were more likely to have positive life outcomes. They were better students, had more refined social skills, earned more money, and were healthier. They were also less likely to abuse drugs, go to jail, or become obese. In short, Mischel's marshmallow work, and several subsequent studies like it, have suggested that a young child's ability to demonstrate self-control has implications that extend well beyond the preschool years, and apply to far more than just marshmallows.

With respect to the role of early educators, Mischel also determined that the "low delayers"—those who couldn't wait for a second marshmallow—could actually learn to become "high delayers." A follow-up brain-imaging study 40 years later revealed visible differences between the two groups in the prefrontal cortex, which, as you'll recall, is the part of the brain that serves as home to the executive function skills, including impulse control.[11] These findings—popularized all the more by the cute videos of kids trying to resist eating that first marshmallow—have grabbed early educators' attention for decades, as they show the potential we have to teach young children self-control strategies and other ME Skills that improve their likelihood of success.

TAKING ME TO THE "STREET"

Right around the time that Mischel began tempting pre-schoolers with marshmallows, *Sesame Street* took to the airwaves, with young children being introduced to this first-of-its-kind preschool programming in 1969. By effectively combining the power of new technology (i.e., television) with education research, *Sesame Street* would go on to become the most widely viewed children's show in the world.[12]

More than 40 years after setting out on their respective journeys, Mischel's marshmallow research made its way to *Sesame Street*. According to Sesame Workshop senior vice president Dr. Rosemarie Truglio,[13] she and her team of early childhood experts recognized the need to focus more attention on helping their preschool audience learn the executive function and self-regulatory skills that Mischel's marshmallows originally brought to light. The character of Cookie Monster seemed perfectly suited for this all-important role, demonstrating just how hard self-control can be while providing children with food for thought.

Recognizing that there was not a simple one-size-fits-all strategy that would work for all children, Sesame Workshop (the non-profit responsible for producing *Sesame Street*) consulted none other than Mischel himself. What resulted was an episode developed specifically to teach preschoolers about self-control and some basic ways to master it, in which Cookie Monster must learn to curb his cookie-devouring impulses to become a member of the "Cookie Connoisseurs Club."[14, 15] Preschoolers who viewed the show segments where Cookie Monster was shown practicing self-control and then participated in a version of the marshmallow test as part of a study conducted by Deborah Linebarger at the University of Iowa's Children's Media Lab were able to resist temptation for longer. This tells us two things: that young children are receptive to and can benefit from being taught ME Skill–related behaviors and strategies; and that the intentional modeling of self-regulatory strategies (including in wide-scale efforts like children's programming) has the potential to help young children "develop stronger executive function skills."[16]

On a follow-up note, *Sesame Street*'s social media team further recognized the opportunity to engage Cookie Monster

> in helping make clear to parents and caregivers of young children the importance of these skills, creating a highly entertaining Cookie Monster version of Icona Pop's song "I Love It" called "Me Want It (But Me Wait)," complete with its own hashtag, #controlmeself.[17] Should you choose to google the video, which I highly recommend, I can all but guarantee you'll find yourself singing along!

ME Skills have continued to prove themselves to be far more than just cute. In 2011, *The Proceedings of the National Academy of Sciences* published an article called "A gradient of childhood self-control predicts health, wealth, and public safety."[18] Authored by a group of highly distinguished researchers from the fields of psychology, neuroscience, psychiatry and the behavioral sciences, and edited by Nobel Prize–winning economist James J. Heckman, the article opened with a ME Skills–related statement of direct relevance to all early educators: "The need to delay gratification, control impulses, and modulate emotional expression is the earliest and most ubiquitous demand that societies place on their children, and success at many life tasks depends critically on children's mastery of such self-control." In this study, researchers used a standard measure of self-control to assess more than a thousand children as young as three years old. As in Mischel's research, follow-up studies decades later revealed that differences in self-control in early childhood predicted a whole range of future life outcomes over the subsequent 30 years, including physical health, drug use, personal finances and criminal offenses.

Regarded as one of the leading researchers in the area of self-control, University of Pennsylvania psychologist Angela Duckworth has similarly focused on the impact these skills have throughout a person's life, likening self-regulation in preschool to resiliency and grit later in life.[19]

Overall, when it comes to the predictive power of self-control, the implications seem increasingly clear: the extent to which young children can put ME Skills into practice matters a lot, not only as it relates to not biting marshmallows (or friends), but also in the long term. It is worth mentioning, however, that the story of Mischel's marshmallows and the seeming consensus around the predictive power of childhood self-control may not yet be fully told. Of note, a modified version of the original marshmallow study was conducted in 2018 by researchers at NYU and UC Irvine.[20] Involving a substantially larger number of preschool test subjects much more broadly representative of the general population than the preschoolers Mischel studied, their findings suggest that it is not just the early development of delayed gratification, but also children's social and economic background that impacts future measures of success.

The ABCs of mindfulness

With all of this talk about self-management and self-control, it might seem like all that's important is for young children to get control of themselves, follow directions, and robotically learn to suppress their emotions. In reality, however, ME Skills are much more dynamic. An equally important aspect of ME Skills is that children need to learn to be more aware of their emotions and how they're feeling so that, over time, they can channel those thoughts and feelings more effectively, productively, and mindfully.

> **Mindfulness:** a mental state achieved by focusing one's awareness on the present moment while calmly acknowledging and accepting one's feelings, thoughts and bodily sensations.[21]

When a child isn't aware of how they feel, controlling or redirecting their big emotions can be practically impossible. It's often children lacking in self-awareness who tend to lash out and act destructively when they feel angry, hurt or jealous. Self-control, self-management and self-restraint can only happen if children learn to identify how they are feeling in the first place. This sort of "emotional literacy" creates the foundation for the WE Skills we'll be discussing in the next chapter, which involve understanding others' emotions. However, children must first become aware of their own feelings before being able to take that next step from ME to WE.

Of course, you can't realistically expect two- and three-year-olds to sit calmly and count to 10 before reacting—it's a good day when you can get a room full of toddlers to sit still for 10 seconds, let alone resist temptation. However, even very young children can learn to pause for a breath and notice their physical sensations. As a teacher, it's understandable that you might be tempted to jump in or react in frustration when a child is having a temper tantrum. But encouraging and helping children practice mindfulness equips them to better manage their emotions. Even small children can benefit from being given (or learning to give themselves) the time and support they need to process what they're feeling, deal with their emotional upsets, and practice self-soothing.

PRACTICALLY MINDFUL

Mindfulness is proving to be an important tool for bridging the gap between young children being aware of how they're feeling and learning how to manage their behavior. A study published in the journal *Developmental Psychology* found that when preschoolers participated in a 12-week program in which they practiced the ABCs of mindfulness—attention, breath and body, and caring—they earned higher marks in academic performance and, more directly pertinent to ME Skills, improved in areas of self-regulation such as emotional and impulse control.[22] As we've discussed, these are not just nice-to-have skills—they are associated with greater success later in life.

As a case in point, my daughter used to have classic two-year-old temper tantrums. Rather than trying to "fix" her feelings, punish her, or send her to her room, my husband and I would (after taking a deep breath ourselves) ask, "Do you need to take some time away?" She would defiantly shout, "Yes!" and march herself up to her room. As she retreated, we would reassure her that we were going to miss her and told her to let us know when she felt better and wanted to rejoin us. Sometimes she'd stay upstairs in her room for quite a long while. When we'd ask whether she was ready to come down, sometimes she'd say no. But, when she was ready, she would come back calmer and more in control of her emotions.

This level of self-awareness and emotional self-control is by no means something to be expected from all young children. (It certainly wasn't the case with our other two.) The point, however, is that giving young children the opportunity, space and support to at least pause, take a deep breath, and regroup—mindfulness in action—is another important way to help foster ME Skills early in life.

IN THE BUSINESS OF ME

As you look to introduce basic mindfulness to preschoolers, be aware that early educators are not the only ones focusing on the promise of mindfulness. In preschool it may come in the form of belly breathing, but mindfulness programs also started becoming more common in the workplace over a decade ago. As Google engineer turned mindfulness guru Bill Duane once explained it, "if business is simply a machine made out of people, mindfulness serves as the WD-40 for the company, lubricating the sticky spots among its many working parts."[23] In the contemporary world of work, as in early education and in life, the ability to pay attention without distraction and to pause and get centered before reacting is of significant value.

DEVELOPMENTAL MILESTONES
The building blocks of ME

There's clearly a lot at stake when it comes to young children's ME Skills development. This makes your role in figuring out how best to understand, recognize and cultivate them in your classroom incredibly valuable. As the neuroscience reinforces for us, the basic development of self-control, self-regulation, self-management and self-awareness (not to mention the development of identity) all start well before age five.

Taking a fresh look at the standard developmental milestones of early childhood, we see when and how young children begin to hone ME Skills.

Milestones

Newborn to six months

From a very young age, babies start to become developmentally capable of an essential element of self-control: self-soothing. Born ready and able to bring their hands to their mouths and suck on them (prenatal ultrasounds sometimes even reveal babies learning to suck their fingers in utero), two-month-olds can, albeit briefly, use this strategy on occasion to calm themselves without the need for any outside intervention. But, for the most part, they are still reliant on caring, responsive adults for calming, whether by talking to them, picking them up, rocking, cooing, singing, or otherwise soothingly engaging with them.

Even very young babies show budding emotional awareness as well, exhibited when they display their ever-so-eagerly anticipated social smile, an expression that over time increasingly conveys emotional meaning. Babies quickly start to become more aware of and adept at expressing their emotions intentionally, for example, employing crying and fussiness to make their feelings known.

Babies are also able to maintain focus and attention during these early months, just not as intently or for as long as they will later in life. Even in the earliest weeks, babies can fix and focus on the faces of their caregivers. By two months, they pay even closer attention to faces and can "fix and follow" objects that are moved across their field of vision.

The gradual disappearance of many of the newborn reflexes—which, by definition, are involuntary and automatic—over the first several months allows babies to start improving their self-control in a physical sense as well. By about four months, they demonstrate their newfound ability to bring their hands across their bodies in front of their faces (described as "crossing midline" in formal milestone lingo) and stare at their amazing discovery. This budding self-awareness, coupled with improving self-control, also leads to babies using their hands and eyes together in a more intentional and coordinated fashion, resulting in fun new abilities such as seeing a toy and successfully reaching for or batting at it.

Six months to one year

Nothing says newfound self-awareness like six-month-olds recognizing themselves in the mirror or responding to their name. Emotions also become easier to recognize, as this is the age when infants characteristically start making sounds that more specifically (and more understandably) convey their joy and displeasure. It is also between six and 12 months when babies develop "joint" or "shared" attention. This ability to intentionally pay attention to or look at the same object as someone else is a particularly important one, as it not only represents an increasing ability to more intentionally direct one's attention, but also their ability to do so in a social way. This shared aspect of joint attention, which by definition involves two people intentionally paying attention to the same thing, makes this both a ME- and a WE-related milestone (which is why you'll find it discussed in the next chapter as well).

DO YOU SEE WHAT I SEE?

In studying the impact that caregivers can have on infants' attention, researchers at Indiana University found a direct connection between how long caregivers looked at an object and how long the infants remained focused on the same object.[24]

One to two years

Twelve-month-olds start to play favorites, whether with toys, books or caregivers. This soon leads to the appearance of temper tantrums characteristic of 18-month-olds, who have a much clearer sense of self, emotions and wants, but who aren't yet skilled at self-management (more commonly identified in early childhood as impulse control). Self-management, you'll recall, is a skill that depends on the prefrontal cortex and executive function skills that don't start picking up in their rate of development until around the age of three.

As children celebrate their first birthdays, they continue to increasingly interact with people and the environment around them and are able to focus for longer periods of time than they could as infants—for example, long enough to follow the path of an object as it falls. This example also illustrates the developing ability to concentrate on objects or people even when they are out of sight, an attention skill first demonstrated by nine-month-olds' characteristic (not to mention endearing) interest in playing peek-a-boo.

In terms of physical self-control, the second year is full of "do-it-myself" firsts, from walking and exploring independently to drinking from a cup and eating with a spoon by the middle of the year. Children round out their second year with increasing independence, which can show itself in the form of defiant behavior (i.e., doing what they want to do rather than what they are told to do).

Three years

Typically by age three, children start using the words "I," "me" and "mine" and grasping their implications. Similarly, the ability to focus and pay attention has developed to the point that they can follow two- or three-step instructions—a milestone that reflects the development of working memory (one of the three defining features of executive function skills). Emerging self-control enables three-year-olds to sit still a bit longer, to concentrate more on activities like listening to stories, copying a circle or building simple three- or four-piece puzzles, and to start to learn to share.

Four years

Finally, four-year-olds typically become less "me-centric," as evidenced by their newfound preference for playing, cooperating, and sharing with other children rather than simply playing next to them. As they increasingly interact with others, it inevitably puts key aspects of their ME Skills, such as impulse control, to the test. They continue to improve their ability to share, wait their turns, and keep their emotions under control. At this age, children may still talk predominantly (sometimes incessantly) about themselves and their interests, while at the same time continually improving in their ability to stop and think through their actions—again drawing on all three components of executive functioning, which as you'll recall include not only impulse control, but also working memory and cognitive flexibility.

STAGE	ME MILESTONES
0–6 months	Self-soothing, emotional awareness and social smile, focus on faces
6–12 months	Increased self-awareness (responds to name, self in mirror)
1–2 years	Clearer sense of self and preferences; increased focus and attention, including "joint" or "shared" attention; "do-it-myself" determination
3 years	"I," "me" and "mine"; emerging self-control
4 years	Continued development of executive functioning, less "me-centric"

CLASSROOM QI-NNECTIONS
What you can do to help ME

As soon as you know what to look for you'll discover that a great many of the typical activities, expectations and daily routines in the early childhood classroom have to do with engaging and encouraging children's ME Skills. Becoming more aware and in control of their emotions as well as their bodies is a key component, while just about all planned activities and games draw to varying degrees on children's abilities to pay attention, follow rules, and have enough control over their impulses to stop, change what they're doing, or let someone else take a turn. This offers you plenty of opportunities throughout the day to help support children's ME Skill development. The following are a few suggestions to get you started.

Activities

- **Be a super model.** Infants, toddlers and preschoolers alike learn best by observing and interacting with the people around them. That means that, from day one, you can look for simple, everyday opportunities to model for children what attention, focus, self-awareness and self-regulation look like. Whether giving babies your undivided attention while feeding them or during diaper changes, using your words to describe how you are feeling, or allowing children to see you pausing to take a few deep, calming breaths when things get a bit harried, you can introduce and reinforce the value of ME Skills in action.

- **Rely on routines.** Routines provide young children with a reassuring sense of security, predictability and comfort—all conditions known to enhance learning. In addition, predictable classroom routines offer children the much-needed chance to practice all of the self-management aspects of ME Skills, control their impulses, and regulate their behavior.

- **Engage in emotional word play.** Managing one's emotions is a cornerstone of ME Skills. Children need first to understand how they're feeling and then learn to put those feelings into words before they can realistically be expected to control their reactions and behaviors. You can help children expand their emotional vocabulary by expanding yours so that they become familiar with and can describe subtle feelings that go beyond simply *happy*, *sad* and *mad*. Consider, for example, introducing (and then explaining) words such as *surprised, frustrated, overwhelmed, confused, relaxed, relieved, proud, brave, concerned* and *excited*. By giving children the words to express themselves in a more meaningful and effective way, this sort of emotional word play can, over time, go a long way towards helping prevent tantrums and other impulsive behaviors.

- **Acknowledge feelings.** When it comes to encouraging children to articulate in their own words what's going on inside, sometimes all it takes is asking, "How are you feeling?" Be careful, however, not to critique children's feelings or explain why they shouldn't feel the way they are feeling. This can be trickier to avoid than it may seem. You may be tempted to try to explain to children why they shouldn't feel a certain way in a well-intentioned attempt to help them feel better about something, but in so doing you run the risk of discouraging their emotional expression and downplaying their emotions. Instead of "Don't be mad," try saying, "I'm sorry you feel that way," or "You seem upset. Can you tell me why?" Whatever you think about their reaction, making sure to acknowledge and sympathize with the very real emotions they are experiencing will put you in a much better position to help them learn new and more acceptable ways of managing their emotions.

- **Try "time away" instead of "time-out."** When a young child resorts to screaming, kicking, biting, or otherwise "losing control," your instinct may be to put them in time-out as punishment to teach them that those behaviors aren't acceptable. As undesirable as these inciting behaviors may be, however, one of the problems with time-outs is that they are generally overshadowed by a significant degree of frustration and anger for everyone involved. These two emotions unfortunately do very little, if anything, to create a positive learning experience. That's why I suggest offering children time away instead. Although this might seem like just another way to refer to time-out, the difference, though subtle, isn't purely semantic, since time away involves a fundamental change in mindset and rationale for using it. Yes, time away still inherently involves children being taken out of or away from environments or situations in which they become overwhelmed or act out. But, rather than being a form of punishment, time away should be seen and treated as a way to give young children the space and time they need to get themselves, their emotions, and their behaviors under better control. Of course, the younger children are, the more likely they will be to need your support in calming themselves down. Should you find your own nerves getting a bit frayed in the process, remind yourself that yelling or getting angry does nothing to calm things down, much less support children's mastery of challenging new social and behavioral skills. After all, even infants are sensitive emotion detectors who will feel the effects of your stress. Instead, take a deep breath and commit to controlling your own emotions as you calmly guide children who are having a hard time away from inciting situations so they can have the space and time to do the same.

WHY TIME-OUTS DON'T ALWAYS WORK OUT

As you look for ways to provide young children with the time and guidance they need to develop ME Skills like self-control and self-management, it helps to remember that "time-out is externally imposed behavior management. It removes the child from the play and does not give practice in expressing feelings, identifying problems, and considering peaceful solutions."[25]

- **Take turns.** Playing games that require turn-taking inherently encourages children to exercise self-control and impulse control, while also offering plenty of opportunity to practice the focus and attention needed to learn to play by the rules. If you think about it, even a simple game you can play with infants, such as peek-a-boo, draws on their developing abilities to focus (in this case on your face and actions) and pay attention (not losing interest as soon as they can't see your face). As children get a bit older, practice can come in the form of something as simple as narrating turn-taking activities, such as alternating stacking blocks by saying, "Now it's your turn" and "Now it's my turn." With preschoolers, playing stop-and-go games such as "Simon Says," "Duck, Duck, Goose," "Red Light, Green Light," "Mother May I," tag and others can all serve to actually make it fun to practice physical self-control, paying close attention, and patiently waiting one's turn.

- **Belly breathing.** You are undoubtedly accustomed to helping young children learn how to point, wave, walk and talk. But how much time do you spend helping them with one of the most basic, yet most important, of all skills—how to breathe? Sure, in a general sense, breathing comes naturally. But learning how to be aware of and even control one's breathing—often put into practice in early childhood circles in the form of "belly breathing" or the popular "in through your nose, out through your mouth" technique—is an effective tool for exercising mindfulness, focusing attention, and managing emotions at any age.

A NEW KIND OF ABCS

Professor Richard Davidson and his team at the Center for Healthy Minds at the University of Wisconsin-Madison have developed techniques for helping preschool teachers introduce a new kind of ABCs based on the mindfulness practices of "Attention, Breathing, and Calming." This includes the valuable skill of self-regulatory breathing,[26] which can be as simple as having children lie on their backs, placing a small (just not choking-hazard small) object on their stomachs, and then watching it rise and fall with each breath. With regular practice, young children can master this calming skill even in the absence of an object, and can then be encouraged to take bigger and deeper breaths to help calm their minds and bodies whenever they feel their emotions start to spiral out of control.

- **Time for transitions.** Transitions, as a fixture of the early childhood classroom, are the in-between times of the day expressly meant to help children learn to more smoothly and efficiently switch mental gears, supporting the development of the "cognitive flexibility" component of executive function skills. This ability to stop what one's doing, follow directions, and move on to something else is a process that typically improves with practice. Helping smooth out these transitions for young children, especially when they haven't yet developed the ability to quickly switch gears, can be as simple as using fun and attention-grabbing cues, chants, puppets, songs, or gentle reminders of what's coming next. This gives them the extra time and encouragement needed to be able to more successfully stop what they're doing and refocus.

- **This is me.** Make time for children to share information about themselves with you and their classmates. They should be encouraged to talk about who they are, where they live, the members of their family, what they like to do, and their favorite foods, for example. Whether you plan a "get to know you" day of sharing in the fall or with each new group of students, or even better, make it a point to routinely have children share something about themselves at various times throughout the year, doing so helps them build self-awareness while at the same time helping you and your students learn more about what makes them who they are.

- **Rest and recess.** Whether you're two, four or 24, self-management skills are at their best when you're well-rested and have had a chance to move your body. If you find children are having regular tantrums or are struggling with self-control in other ways (such as hitting, biting, throwing or kicking), ask about how they're sleeping at night, and consider how they've been napping and whether they're getting enough physical activity during the day. Remember, there's a learning curve when it comes to putting ME Skills into practice, and it is well-recognized that physical activity and being well-rested can go a long way toward helping children flex their mental muscles. Of note, it has been shown that executive functions suffer first and foremost when children do not get enough sleep, making it all the harder for them to think clearly or exercise good self-control.[27]

- **Be mindful yourself.** Remember to practice paying attention to the here and now yourself, both in and outside of your classroom. Not only can it help you deal with the inevitable stressors and distractions in your day, but it has also been shown that children benefit from teachers who are mindfully present.[28]

THE PURPOSE BEHIND MINDFULNESS
Mindfulness involves "paying attention in a particular way: on purpose, in the present moment, and nonjudgmentally."[29]

JON KABAT-ZINN
father of the mindfulness movement

- **See the ME in story time.** If there's one thing that all of the sitting, thinking, listening, taking turns, asking questions, and sharing ideas typical of story time all have in common, it's that they require a whole lot from young children in the way of focus, attention, and self-management. This makes story time about much more than reading books: it represents a great opportunity to recognize, encourage, and praise children as they practice their ME Skills. Remember that mastering these skills takes time, so be understanding when young children's underdeveloped self-control manifests itself in an inability to sit still, keep their hands to themselves, or stay seated.

- **Calming corner.** While the words "calming" and "corner" seem to go perfectly well together, there's nothing particularly special or intuitive about this coupling. In fact, for some, sitting in a corner has a negative effect. Instead, focus on creating a designated area or spaces in your classroom where you can best facilitate the calming of children's big emotions and feelings. When possible, think about making available objects that are likely to have a calming effect, such as plush toys, squeeze toys and comfy chairs, and create a relaxed area and ambience, perhaps by playing quiet music. Basically, your goal should be to create a "low-stress" safe space meant to help young children refocus, relax, and engage their ME Skills.

QI TAKEAWAYS: ME

- ME Skills are the inward-facing self-awareness and self-management skills that allow us to be in control of our thoughts, feelings and actions.

- ME is not the same as "me." Rather than self-centeredness or any of the negative connotations associated with being self-involved, ME Skills represent important self-management skills associated with lifelong success.

- ME Skills are not just about self-control: they also include things such as emotional self-awareness and the development of identity and a strong, healthy sense of self.

- ME Skills are foundational for the development and fostering of all other QI Skills.

QI REFLECTIONS: ME

- Look around (or picture) your classroom. Consider what, if any, areas, activities or objects you have in the classroom that could lend themselves well to helping children calm down and better self-regulate.

- Think about—and better yet, write down—a couple of recent challenges that children in your class faced. Now, consider whether or how they might have been the result of not-yet-fully developed ME Skills. How did you respond? How did the children involved respond? In retrospect, think about how well your actions served as a model for or supported the development of your student's ME Skills. What else could you do in such situations to lend children use of your executive function skills?

- Think about instances where you're more likely to be stressed or have difficulty regulating your own emotions. What triggers these emotions? What have you done to regain your composure? Do you apply these approaches to how you handle stress in your classroom, and model them for your students?

WE
Learning to Play
Well with Others

. . . .

"Relationships are the defining
feature of being human. Social relationships
are one of the most important forms of
experience that literally form who we are."[30]

DR. DAN SIEGEL

F EVER there were a set of skills that captured the essence of preschool, it would be the skills required to "play well" with others. Learning to "put your listening ears on," "use your words," take turns, share, and acknowledge others' feelings represent but a few examples of the type of interpersonal or relational skills that are taught in early childhood classrooms. As easy as they may be to see, however, not everyone recognizes just how valuable what I call WE Skills are—not just for getting along, but for learning.

Sure, every teacher and parent wants their children to learn to play well with and be nice to others. But the benefits of these social skills extend well beyond the classroom, and the impact is long-lasting. Don't just take my word for it: ask any adult you know whether they believe that skills such as communication, collaboration, teamwork, active listening, empathy and perspective-taking play a useful role in their personal or professional lives. I'm pretty darn confident you'll find—as I have over my many years of discussing QI Skills with audiences ranging from preschool teachers to global business leaders—that given a moment to reflect on how key these are to our lives, we can all see the inherent value of WE Skills.

Given that it's highly unlikely you need convincing that these skills are important, the plan for this chapter is instead to help you draw meaningful connections between WE Skills in their easy-to-recognize and fully developed adult form, and the ways in which they typically present themselves in foundational stages of development. We'll also cover, of course, what you can do to embrace and help bring them to life in your classrooms.

My hope is that by the end of this chapter you'll realize just how meaningful an opportunity you have, through your everyday interactions with young children, to teach, model, share, facilitate and nurture this coveted category of skills that are so key for life success.

> 💜 **WE Skills** are the "relationship" and "people" skills necessary for effective communication, collaboration and teamwork. They involve emotional intelligence, social-emotional skills, active listening, empathy, perspective-taking, and the ability to play well with others.

What are WE Skills?

In the most intuitive sense of the word "we," WE Skills are *people* skills. They're all about forming relationships and interacting with others. WE Skills are a natural extension of ME Skills. This may not seem immediately obvious, but as you'll recall, ME Skills are inner-facing and all about the self: *self*-awareness, *self*-control, *self*-regulation and *self*-management. WE Skills represent, in a sense, the outward-facing equivalent. They involve the tools necessary to understand how and why other people think, feel and act the way they do. When you think about it this way, it makes good sense that young children would need to gain crucial ME Skills, such as the ability to recognize, understand, name and control their own emotions, as well as learn to focus and pay attention, before becoming skilled at relating to and interacting with others.

WE Skills defined

WE Skills are most notably represented by the following abilities:

- Communication
- Collaboration
- Teamwork
- Empathy
- Emotional intelligence
- Social-emotional skills
- Active listening
- Perspective-taking

"Every human being needs to listen consciously
in order to live fully connected in space
and in time to the physical world around us,
connected in understanding to each other."[31]

JULIAN TREASURE
"Five Ways to Listen Better," *TEDGlobal*, July 2011

WE Skills serve as the critical foundation for relationships and connectedness. They are what make it possible for us to listen to, better understand, communicate and interact with, relate well to, and consider others' points of view. In other words, they give us the ability to read other people.

Calling them "soft skills" doesn't do them justice or capture their central importance to success in our relationships, work, and life in general. As you think of a WE-Skilled adult, rather than picturing someone who's a bit "soft," imagine instead a superb communicator who listens attentively and is particularly skilled at reading other people and building and maintaining strong, diverse relationships. This is a person who is able to handle new challenges with confidence. Strong WE Skills have been shown to also improve academic performance (IQ Skills), and parents, pediatricians and employers alike are joining educators in recognizing that WE Skills are, now more than ever, a "must-have."

> In school and in life, it is as important to be able to read other people as it is to read.

ME and WE

If all this talk about ME and WE Skills makes you think of the term "emotional intelligence," there's a good reason why. It is, in fact, the powerful combination of ME and WE that captures and conveys the essence of emotional intelligence, which is described as the capacity to be aware of, control, and express one's emotions, and to handle interpersonal relationships judiciously and empathetically.

THE RISE OF EI

Emotional intelligence, or EI, rose to global prominence in the 1990s thanks in large part to former *New York Times* brain and sciences reporter Daniel Goleman. From his 1995 best-selling book *Emotional Intelligence: Why It Can Matter More Than IQ* to his subsequent work as an internationally renowned psychologist, Goleman contributed greatly to solidifying the business world's interest in, understanding, and valuing of the same sorts of skills you're helping to foundationally develop in your classrooms each day.

In close alignment with emotional intelligence is social and emotional learning (SEL). The championing of evidence-based educational SEL practices by organizations such as CASEL (the Collaborative for Academic, Social, and Emotional Learning), which we learned about in the previous chapter, has contributed to the significant rise of SEL. This put SEL and, by association, ME and WE Skills in the educational spotlight even before the COVID-19 pandemic further showcased their importance. As of 2022, more than 90% of schools and districts in the U.S. reported focusing their efforts on the development of students' SEL skills.[32]

As it relates to early childhood education, SEL (which encompasses both ME and WE Skills) now features prominently in a wide range of "whole child" and "kindergarten readiness" efforts, right alongside teaching the ABCs and 123s. Pediatricians, too, look for this type of development. In 2022, the American Academy of Pediatrics (AAP) and

Centers for Disease Control and Prevention (CDC) revised their gold-standard checklist of children's developmental milestones to, among other things, more formally emphasize the importance of healthy social-emotional development during the early years.[33, 34]

As it did for ME Skills, CASEL offers a very useful definition of SEL as a process that involves the WE Skill–related development of *feeling and showing empathy* and *relationship-building*. The organization's CASEL 5 framework lends additional support to the fact that ME and WE Skills combined capture not only the essence of emotional intelligence, but also social-emotional learning. While self-awareness and self-management, along with responsible decision-making, serve as the framework's ME Skill–relevant aspects, the other two skills rounding out the CASEL 5—social awareness and relationship skills—clearly align with WE.

SEL DEFINED

Social and emotional learning (SEL), which has come to be recognized as both an intuitive and integral part of education and human development, is defined as a "process through which individuals learn and apply a set of social, emotional, and related skills, attitudes, behaviors, and values that help direct their thoughts, feelings, and actions in ways that enable them to succeed in school, work and life"[35]

One thing I hope the definitions of SEL and emotional intelligence make clear is that getting the cultivation of QI Skills right is not simply a matter of moving beyond ME to WE.

Nor is it just about recognizing the importance of ME Skills only in terms of how they inform WE. ME Skills and WE Skills are each valuable in their own right. Together they prove to be a winning combination.

WE in early childhood

In the early years, WE Skills can be broken down into their foundational, intuitive forms of language, listening, and understanding others' emotions. These are, after all, the skills that enable young children to learn to play nice, communicate, make friends and share.

When it comes to making the case for how much these WE Skills, in their earliest form, stand to influence children's future life outcomes for the better, consider the following. In a study conducted by my Penn State colleagues, who are regarded as some of the top social-emotional researchers in the country, kindergarten teachers were asked to rate various social and communication (in other words, WE-related) skills. Points were given based on qualities such as "cooperates with peers," "shares materials," "is helpful to others," "is very good at understanding feelings," and "resolves problems on their own." When researchers checked in on these five-year-old test subjects nearly 20 years later, they found that for every one-point increase in original scores, the children were:

- 54% more likely to have earned a high school diploma.

- Twice as likely to have attained a college degree in early adulthood.

- Nearly 50% more likely to have a full-time job at age 25.

They were also found to be less likely to use drugs, have had run-ins with the juvenile justice system, or have experienced mental health issues.[36] As I've traveled around speaking to wide-ranging audiences, I've found that real-world results like these do a particularly good job of opening people's eyes to the importance of all of these "plays well with others" skills. Of course, I've found it worth noting that studies like these don't simply reflect the key role of kindergarten and kindergarten teachers in helping kids develop these skills: they show us that we should make this a priority in how we raise and teach young children long before they ever reach elementary school age.

WHAT HAPPENS IN EARLY CHILDHOOD DOESN'T STAY IN EARLY CHILDHOOD

In a Penn State University study of disadvantaged children, five-year-olds with better social skills—such as cooperating, listening, and helping others—were more likely to graduate high school, get a college degree, and be gainfully employed in their 20s. They were also less likely to have issues with the juvenile justice system, substance abuse, or mental health.[37] The findings provide one more compelling example of how early skill development lays a foundation that children will build upon for the rest of their lives.

Language and listening skills, core components of WE Skills that develop even earlier than the five-year-old social and communication skills measured by my Penn State colleagues, also play a foundational role in setting young children up for success. At first glance, these may seem a bit like ME Skills.

It is true, for example, that hearing could technically be considered an inward-facing cognitive process, as it requires one's attention, focus, and brainpower to receive and process sound. However, hearing is not the same thing as listening, which is relationship-based. As such, the latter represents a WE Skill that is crucial for effective communication. Just think of the phrase, "I know you can hear me, but are you *listening* to me?" Listening is the social application of hearing: it's a two-way street that requires us to actually comprehend and make sense of not only the words, but also the emotions and intent behind what someone else is saying. Similarly, when it comes to language, the ability to speak and "use your words" may well start out as an individual ME Skill, but it's also the necessary foundation upon which children can more outwardly and relationally build the key WE abilities of communicating, sharing ideas, and connecting with and relating to others.

IN THE BUSINESS OF WE:
RELATIONSHIPS MATTER

It could be said that today's business world has gone "soft" (in a good way) with regard to its newfound emphasis on interpersonal skills. Solid social skills and the ability to work in a team and distinguish oneself as a "people person" are now some of the traits most sought after by employers. This shift is not all that surprising when you consider just how globally complex and connected the world of work has become. Employees must be able to relate to, understand, and communicate effectively with not only coworkers in other departments and clients or partners at other companies, but also with colleagues and customers on other continents and from different cultures—even if they never actually meet on the same side of a screen.

No matter the industry, everyone must bring WE Skills to the table to be effective, innovative and productive. As LinkedIn co-founder Reid Hoffman has aptly put it, in today's world "an individual's power is raised exponentially with the help of a team."[38] In fact, it's one of his company's stated core values: "Relationships matter."

DEVELOPMENTAL MILESTONES
Getting acquainted with WE milestones

It's easy to see WE Skills taking root very early. All babies are born with a drive to relate, connect and learn from others. Some of the most revealing modern baby-brain research examines the earliest forms of foundational learning: language and communication. The development of these skills is impressively, if not entirely, socially dependent. Social interactions with caring, responsive adults are what trigger babies' brains to become sponges for knowledge—so much so that interactions with caring, responsive adults have been characterized as the social switch that turns on learning.[39] When you interact with young children, you're helping build and shape their brains in ways that enable them to develop even stronger WE Skills in the future.

Given that social interactions are the basis upon which baby brains develop, you'll find that they are therefore well represented in the developmental milestones of WE Skills. The following are some key WE-related milestones you can watch for and help children master throughout the first five years.

Milestones

Two months
By two months of age, babies have started to master the social smile in response to your talking to or smiling at them. Two-month-olds turn their heads attentively toward sounds, calm down when spoken to or picked up, and seem happy to see you.

Four months
Babies at this age not only routinely smile at people spontaneously, but will also do so to get your attention. If need be, they'll go to additional lengths to achieve this end—moving, looking at you, or making sounds. More than just attention-seeking, however, four-month-olds enjoy interacting and playing with others, and respond to affection that comes their way with smiles and coos. They copy other people's expressions and sounds and, in applying what they hear, soon begin to babble.

Six months

In a show of budding social competence and emotional matura-
tion, typical six-month-olds like to take part in such socially
motivated activities as "blowing raspberries"—putting their
tongue between their lips and forcing air (and, oftentimes,
spit bubbles) out of their mouths; laughing; and making
squealing noises. They also become better two-way com-
municators, using gestures that include facial expressions,
actions, and sounds to respond to others; and engaging in
"conversations" by taking turns making sounds in response
to those they hear from other people. Their ability to recognize familiar people also improves.

Nine months

In a fun display of increasing social interaction and budding
language development, infants at this age are known for
their endearing ability to make recognizable sounds, including "mama," "dada" and "baba." Nine-month-olds hone their
ability to identify (and respond differently) to familiar versus
unfamiliar people. This is a social skill that comes in handy,
but may at times cause them to act shy, fearful and clingy
around strangers.

Nine-month-olds also develop an important ability called
"shared attention," which is also referred to as "joint attention"
or "gaze shifting." As you may recall from the ME chapter, joint attention is what allows infants to share a common
focus on something, such as a person or object—for example, if you look at a book, they follow your gaze and turn
their attention to the same book. Joint attention is a critical
skill that's now considered to be at the heart of language
development, because it allows nine-month-olds to understand what you're directing their attention to as you point
to things and name them.

DO YOU SEE WHAT I SEE?

The seemingly simple but fundamentally social ability of infants to follow the gaze of an adult to see what they're looking at—often referred to as "joint" or "shared" attention—has been positively correlated with all sorts of future abilities that are dependent on shared experiences and knowledge. These include measures of language abilities as toddlers,[40] and expand into mastery of a wide range of cultural conventions and social skills.[41]

12 months

As children round out their first year they become all the more social, playing interactive games like pat-a-cake and waving bye-bye. They also make progress in their understanding of verbal instructions—starting with "no," which may only result in their briefly pausing whatever they're doing, but still stopping long enough to demonstrate their understanding.

15 months

Language and communication skills continue to grow. Fifteen-month-olds typically expand their vocabulary beyond just "mama" or "dada" to include a couple of additional words, such as "ball" and "dog." This may come out as "ba" and "da," but what they're trying to communicate is still clear. Understanding also improves at this age, as children are generally able to follow directions given with both words and gestures. With respect to empathy and perspective-taking, this is the age when children start paying closer attention to and even copying what other children are doing, showing others things they themselves like, and showing affection to both people and things they like through their cuddles, hugs and kisses.

18 months

Lots of new interactions and shared understanding takes place at 18 months. Following one-step commands, pointing to show you things of interest, and working with you to tackle such toddlerhood-defining tasks as dressing or handwashing are all typical of this age. So is an 18-month-old's willingness to separate from you or a parent, though they often still want familiar adults close by for reassurance.

GOLDFISH CRACKERS, BROCCOLI, AND TODDLER EMPATHY

In a simple yet poignant study, toddlers were shown two bowls of food. The first contained goldfish crackers, chosen because of their near-universal toddler appeal; the other, some notably less toddler-tempting broccoli. Before handing over the bowls, an experimenter ate from each and proceeded to act as if she either loved the goldfish and was disgusted by the broccoli or just the opposite— loved the broccoli and hated the goldfish. The toddlers were then given access to both bowls.

Upon being asked by the experimenter, "Could I have some?" the 14-month-old participants shared with the experimenter some beloved goldfish crackers, regardless of how the experimenter had reacted to them. The

18-month-olds, however, did something different. In what turned out to be a revealing show of understanding that someone else might actually want something different from what they themselves would want, these slightly older toddlers responded to the experimenter's question by handing over whichever food the experimenter had liked.

As the researchers concluded, this showed that the basic impulses of children as young as 18 months can not just guide them towards empathy, but also lead them beyond empathy to sharing and genuine altruism—one goldfish cracker or stalk of broccoli at a time.[42]

Two years
From a social-emotional development standpoint, two-year-olds are likely to notice when others are feeling upset or hurt, even pausing or looking sad when someone else is crying. As a sign of their improving emotional literacy, they will also now look to you (or, more accurately, at your face) to see how to react to a new situation. The ability to put at least two words together helps them better verbally communicate, as does their use of an expanded range of gestures that go beyond just waving and pointing, including blowing kisses and nodding yes.

Two-and-a-half years
Whereas children tend to engage mostly in "parallel" play up to this age, now is the time when they start to become more social in the way they interact and play, choosing to play *with* other children rather than just alongside them. They can also say about 50 words, including "we" (in addition to

"I" and "me"), which greatly improves their ability to communicate and relate to others.

Three years
In preschoolers, WE Skills really start to blossom. This makes sense from a developmental standpoint, as children practice applying their much more rapidly developing social abilities. These include noticing and being much more likely to join other children playing, talking well enough that they can be understood by others (at least most of the time), and the ability to better engage in back-and-forth conversations.

Four years
At four, children gain a better grasp of language and communication with the ability to string together longer and more meaningful sentences (four or more words); recite some of the words from songs, stories or nursery rhymes; and talk about or share with a parent or caregiver at least one thing that happened during their day.

At this age, children also become more adept at perspective-taking with dress-up and make-believe play, as they pretend to be "Mom," "Dad," and other familiar figures in their lives. Interactive games are especially appealing to most four-year-olds, who would often rather play with others than by themselves—so much so at this age that they'll actively seek out other children to play with. As four-year-olds spend more time playing with other children they also demonstrate an increased ability to empathize, routinely comforting others who are hurt or sad.

STAGE	WE MILESTONES
2 months	social smile, early active listening
4 months	smile, coo, copy expressions and sounds
6–12 months	babble, body language and play, increasing social sense, shared (joint) attention
1–2 years	budding communication skills, increasing awareness of or interest in wants, needs and feelings of others
3–5 years	rapidly developing social abilities (use your words, take turns, play nice, share), pretend play, empathy and perspective-taking

CLASSROOM QI-NNECTIONS
Encouraging WE Skills in a wee world

In a highly connected world, one's WE Skill-cultivating capabilities become more important than ever. Perhaps the most important thing you can do to help foster young children's WE Skills is to provide plenty of opportunities for them to witness WE Skills in action and practice them. Remember that, just as with learning to read, learning how to read other people is an equally complicated process that takes lots of time, practice, mistakes, and the opportunity to learn from those mistakes. Young children are still in the process of learning how emotions work and how to get along with each other, so although it's good to encourage them to practice their WE Skills, it's equally important to not expect perfection. You can help children develop WE Skills through modeling the behaviors you want to see, talking them through it when they make "mistakes," and creating valuable learning experiences, such as those listed below, to get you started.

....

"Emotional literacy is not just a gift; it's actually an ability that can be taught to our children, starting when they are young as toddlers . . . The seeds are planted even earlier, by how we relate and respond to our infants."

MICHELLE BORBA
Unselfie: Why Empathetic Kids Succeed in Our All-About-Me World

....

Activities

- **Encourage active listening.** The better children become at active listening, the better they become at both learning from and interacting with others. You can start encouraging this important aspect of WE Skills by:

  - **Setting a sound example.** Simply model attentive listening yourself. Whether by listening to and then responding to a baby's cries and coos, a toddler's babble or a preschooler's chatter, your daily demonstrations of active listening will go a long way toward helping them learn to do the same. As part of your efforts, remember to set aside distractions, minimize multi-tasking, and commit to offering your undivided attention whenever possible.

• **Helping children put their listening ears on.** Taking turns talking, as with all turn-taking, inherently involves both ME and WE Skills. This includes the relational aspect of taking turns that factors in not just what you want to say, but also what others want to say. Refraining from interrupting requires impulse control and active listening. As a great active listening practice, you can borrow from the *Tools of the Mind*[43] playbook and help or have children make note cards— one with a picture of a pair of lips, and the other with an ear. They can hold these up and pass them around to each other during group activities as tangible cues or reminders of when it's their turn to speak (mouth card) and listen (ear card).

• **Check the emotional climate or your classroom.** Make sure that each child entering your classroom gets to start their day with a warm welcome. Get down at their level to greet them when they come in and ask about how they're feeling. This models and reinforces key WE concepts while sending the message, "I see you, I hear you, and I'm glad you're here." Do this routinely, just as you check regularly to see how children are mastering their ABCs and 123s. Make time for quick but meaningful emotional check-ins throughout each day to show children you care how they're feeling.

EMOTIONS, LEARNING, AND THE BRAIN

As you go about your day, remember that each student's emotional state on any given day stands to play a significant a role in their ability to learn. In fact, key research compiled in the book *Emotions, Learning and the Brain: Exploring the Educational Implications of Affective Neuroscience* by Mary Helen Immordino-Yang confirms that not only are emotions powerful motivators of learning, but also that it is neurobiologically impossible to build memories, engage in complex thoughts, or make meaningful decisions in the absence of emotions![44]

- **Make story time relatable.** Remember that the value of having young children listen to stories isn't just about them sitting still and passively listening to the words, but also about their relating to the characters and the story. As an easy way to boost the WE Skill benefits of reading, encourage young children to comment on and ask and answer questions about stories, and discuss how various characters might be feeling.

- **Use *your* words.** In early childhood, as in life, learning to use one's words helps improve a child's ability to communicate and "play well" with others, whereas the inability to communicate ideas, wants, needs, frustrations or emotions all too often results in less socially tolerated behaviors such as hitting, biting, and throwing objects or tantrums. By simply using *your* words, you can help young children more effectively use theirs, and start to learn how to read other people. Make it a habit to comment on or put into words both how you're feeling and what you think they are feeling, taking time to ask clarifying questions such as, "Are you upset because you wanted to read another book?" As their vocabularies grow, provide them with the words and opportunities to use those words to help with the constructive communication aspect of WE Skills development.

- **Practice "playing nice."** It has long been said that play is the "work" of three-year-olds. This is true for many reasons, not the least of which is the fact that this is the age when children begin making leaps and bounds in their understanding of, showing affection for, and interacting with other children. That's not to say that the shift from individual (or parallel) play characteristic of one- and two-year-olds to the more interactive, social play of three-year-olds happens smoothly and overnight; it takes plenty of practice. But affording plenty of playtime (especially in the context of an age-appropriate supervised early childhood classroom) offers young children ample opportunities to put their budding listening, language, sharing, turn-taking, and empathy skills into practice.

- **Walk in someone else's shoes.** This concept—which was even expressly encouraged by a former President of the United States[45]—is what young children practice doing every day. As popular preschool pastimes, dress-up and role-play give young children the chance to put themselves literally and figuratively in others' shoes. When pretending to be someone else, they're practicing perspective-taking. When they imagine what it would be like to think, feel, talk and act like someone else, they're strengthening their ability to understand where someone else is coming from. Even just making a few dress-up supplies available in your classroom can go a long way toward getting the ball rolling by helping children to imagine creative scenarios—whether that's playing school, doctor or house—and strengthening the early roots of empathy and perspective-taking.

"The biggest deficit that we have in our society and the world right now is an empathy deficit. We are in great need of people being able to stand in somebody else's shoes and see the world through their eyes."

PRESIDENT BARACK OBAMA

- **Demonstrate reading (and responding to) body language.** By simply being an attentive caregiver who notices and is responsive to young children's hand and body movements, you can help children learn to become aware of and interpret other people's emotions, intentions and perspective, even in the absence of words. Because infants first learn how to respond to others by watching the adults in their lives, it's never too early to make a point of carefully observing and responding to babies' physical movements and other non-verbal cues. As soon as you commit to looking for these early signs of WE, you discover that even infants use natural signals to communicate. Infants who smack their lips may be hungry, while those who turn their heads away are less likely to be. Toddlers who cover their faces or turn their backs are usually trying to tell you something. And how a preschooler is feeling is written (often in exaggerated fashion) all over their faces.

- **Read the signs.** Months before young children can actually speak, they are able to master the motor skills necessary for what can be described as more "manual" modes of communication, including meaningful gesturing such as waving and pointing as well as the more formal movements that constitute sign language. Typical 12- to 18-month-olds' spoken vocabulary is limited to a handful of words, but babies as young as six to nine months possess the motor skills to start learning how to sign, and are soon able to communicate an impressively wide range of practical concepts such as *eat, sleep, more milk, book, diaper, please, thank you, mom, dad,* and *all done.* This makes baby sign language a particularly fun and interactive way to help with early WE Skill development. What's more, teaching babies sign language is believed to actually help, rather than interfere with, the development of verbal language. If the idea of learning sign language seems a bit daunting, rest assured there are plenty of books and apps that can help turn it into a fun and hands-on communication enhancing experience for everyone involved—including you!

- **Make helping others routine.** At the heart of getting along well with people is being kind and caring. Even very young toddlers come by this skill naturally, showing concern or offering a hug (or some goldfish crackers or broccoli) to others. So one of your most important roles, other than just modeling kind and caring behavior, is to make sure young children have daily opportunities to practice thinking about doing things for someone other than themselves. Early on, this can be as simple as praising a toddler who shows sympathy or concern for someone who is upset, or recognizing a preschooler who shares a toy with a friend. As children get a bit older, consider additional ways students can meaningfully participate in helping others, like collecting canned goods or coins to donate to charity.

> "Alone we can do so little;
> together we can do so much."
>
> **HELEN KELLER**

- **Ask, "How would you feel?"** Having children think about how others might feel and imagine "being in their shoes" is fundamentally important, and not just in the heat of the moment when they've impulsively hit or snatched a toy from someone else. Children should be encouraged to regularly stop and think about this in the context of the golden rule—teaching them to treat others as they want to be treated. This is also a great question to ask in general (for instance, while reading books), because it will reinforce how important you think it is to pay attention to other people's feelings in addition to mastering one's own.

- **Read with feeling.** Books are excellent tools for building vocabulary, literacy, and active listening skills and improving emotional literacy. Even babies can read emotions on faces, which is why they tend to respond well to books featuring faces. When reading together, be sure to point out characters' emotions, helping children learn to look for and become skilled at recognizing a wide range of them. Fortunately, the fact that even young children have very BIG feelings means, among other things, that there are lots of good books about feelings for you to read.

- **Sing, sing a song.** Children's songs like "If You're Happy and You Know It" provide a great way to introduce, reinforce, and have fun teaching children about emotions.

When you sing and act out the simple verses of "If You're Happy and You Know It," you are reinforcing (and putting into words and actions) the concept of being happy, what a happy face looks like, and that faces in general are important for conveying emotions. But you don't need to stop there: take the opportunity to introduce other motions and emotions. Swap out "clap your hands" for "stomp your feet" as you replace "happy" with "sad." Then try "surprised" and so on. Make up as many representative faces or actions as you like. As your students catch on, let them be the ones to suggest new, more challenging emotions to act out.

QI TAKEAWAYS: WE

- WE Skills are outward-facing people skills that allow us to understand how and why other people think, feel, and act the way they do.

- WE Skills and ME Skills create a powerful combination that encompasses both emotional intelligence (EI) and social-emotional learning (SEL).

- As a defining aspect of WE, it is as important for children to learn to read other people as it is for them to learn to read.

- The ability to put on one's listening ears, use one's words, and play well with others is not just child's play: these WE-defining skills have proven themselves to be valuable at every age, all the way from the playroom to the boardroom.

QI REFLECTIONS: WE

- Think of a time when you truly felt seen or heard by someone else. What did they do to make you feel that way?

- Take a moment to consider how well you know the emotional climate in your classroom. What could you do to better read the room and attend to your students' emotions? What could you do to make sure you truly connect with your students at the start of each day?

- Reflect on a recent day in your classroom, focusing on the interactions you have with your students and those they have with each other. Make a list of specific interactions, both positive and challenging, and think about how each could serve as a WE Skill learning or teaching opportunity.

?

WHY
Seeing the World as
a Question Mark

· · · · · · · · · · · · · · · · · · · ·

"The important thing is not to stop questioning.
Curiosity has its own reason for existing."
ALBERT EINSTEIN

"Welcome to the era of the curious leader, where
success may be less about having all the answers
and more about wondering and questioning."
WARREN BERGER
author of *A More Beautiful Question: The*
Power of Inquiry to Spark Breakthrough Ideas

FIRST BABIES COO. Then, they babble. From there, the words start flowing. If you stop to think about it, it takes surprisingly little time—a few years at most—from when children utter their first, eagerly anticipated words to the point where you can expect to be all but besieged by a single, highly significant, yet at times exasperating word. If you're thinking that the one particular word I'm referring to is "no," that would certainly qualify as a reasonable guess, but one to save for a different discussion. The word I'm referring to, as evidenced by the title of this chapter, is *why*. This ever-so-frequently repeated word inevitably finds its way into just about every young child's vocabulary (some more than others).

Yet this desire to ask why represents something much bigger and more important than just a new three-letter word in a child's growing vocabulary or, for that matter, a challenge to your authority. It represents the fundamentally important act of questioning that helps us better understand the world around us.

> **?** **WHY Skills,** which include questioning, curiosity, inquisitiveness and wonder, are the discovery-related skills that help us better understand how the world works. They involve asking not just why, but all sorts of other questions in order to further one's understanding.

What is WHY?

If we were to take the term strictly at face value, we might think we could just define WHY Skills as the asking of a fairly simple question (or line of questioning) and call it a day. But there's actually a bit more to WHY Skills than meets the eye.

As a foundational QI Skill, WHY involves asking all sorts of questions about how the world works. It's a demonstration of inquisitiveness and curiosity in myriad forms, which includes asking not only *who*, *what*, *when* and *where*, but also the more probing questions of *why* and *how*. Collectively, WHY Skills represent the fundamental thirst for knowledge and understanding that both motivates young children to explore the world around them (thus facilitating the connecting of neurons in their developing brains) and serves to define an ageless and invaluable aspect of human nature. WHY Skills comprise several core attributes:

- Questioning
- Curiosity
- Inquisitiveness
- Wonder

In the chapters to follow, we'll also be exploring how WHY Skills drive WILL, WIGGLE and WOBBLE and ultimately facilitate WHAT IF Skills—the ability to question at a deeper, more creative level and explore not just how the world *is* but also imagine how it *could be*. For the purposes of this chapter, we're going to cover the WHY basics, as well as dig a bit deeper—asking (and answering) a few clarifying questions about WHY, starting with the fundamental question, "Why ask why?"

> "Knowing the answers will help you in school.
> Knowing how to question will help you in life."[46]
>
> **WARREN BERGER**

Why ask why?

It was during the time when I was first working to create the QI Skill framework and asking myself how I might bring to people's attention the value of asking questions that I first learned about a popular training technique developed by an engineer at Toyota called the "Five Whys." Well-known in the business world, the Five Whys is an "iterative question-asking technique meant to promote deep thinking through questioning."[47] True to its name, the technique involves asking "why" five times for the purpose of getting to the root of problems and finding meaningful answers. Why five? Good question. After asking myself the same thing, I googled it, and apparently five was simply the number originally deemed sufficient for the job. Of course, in some instances asking even more "whys" can prove beneficial, so there's no reason to limit this type of exploration.

In any case, the strategy is meant to encourage and facilitate deeper exploration of cause-and-effect relationships and has been adopted by some of the world's most innovative companies.[48, 49]

"So what?" you ask. "What exactly does that have to do with me or the young children I teach?" Allow me to answer with a thought-provoking question in return: Why is it that companies should have to go to such great lengths and spend significant time and money to train adults—high-level businesspeople, no less—to do something that anyone who has ever spent any time engaging with young children knows they do so naturally?

This is the question that really got me thinking about the importance of WHY Skills, and I hope it's now started you thinking more deeply about them as well. With the ability to ask lots of good questions proving itself to be invaluable in today's world, this chapter is going to focus on two equally important WHY Skill questions:

1   What role do you, as early educators, stand to play in nurturing and strengthening children's developing WHY Skills?

2   How can you avoid inadvertently training young children to ignore their WHY instincts?

WHY: IT'S GOOD FOR BUSINESS

Being curious naturally involves WHY Skills and the ability to ask probing questions. It isn't all that surprising that questioning and curiosity—which are central to so many valued skills in an AI-powered world—have become a prominent theme in business, leadership, entrepreneurship and, of course, innovation. For example:

- In the words of Dell founder Michael Dell, "Curiosity can inspire [the seeking out of] fresh ideas and approaches needed to keep pace with change"—a concept reinforced in a survey of 1,000 CEOs that identified curiosity as one of the most important leadership traits.[50]

- According to LinkedIn founder Reid Hoffman, the constant asking of "why" is one of the defining features of entrepreneurs.

- Globally acclaimed businessman and philanthropist Ratan Tata attested to just how central WHY Skills are to innovation by recognizing innovators' inherent need to "question the unquestionable."

- Harvard Business School professor Clayton Christensen notes that innovators are consummate questioners who show a passion for inquiry. Based on his study of how people come up with groundbreaking ideas, he identified questioning as one of five key discovery skills, emphasizing that what all innovators have in common is that they constantly ask provocative questions and "leave few rocks unturned."[51]

Questions vs. Answers

In today's Information Age, the value of rote memorization is plummeting while the value of being able to ask insightful questions and pursue answers is rapidly increasing. In one sense, educators have always valued (or at least claimed to value) children's questioning "reflex"—a belief captured in the mantra, "There's no such thing as a stupid question." Yet it's one thing to say you value questioning, and another to actually prioritize this belief in daily practice.

THE VALUE OF A QUESTION

Albert Einstein famously said, "If I had an hour to solve a problem and my life depended on the solution, I would spend the first 55 minutes determining the proper question to ask. For once I know the proper question, I could solve the problem in less than five minutes."

Treating the world as a question mark

So, what does it look like when young children treat the world as a question mark?[52] In theory, it sounds great: young children eager to explore and learn, toddling around touching, tasting, pointing, and asking "Why?" and "What's that?" In reality, however, this kind of curiosity-in-action involves young children getting into everything and—as they master the skill—questioning rules, instructions, and requests in a way that, to some, can feel like an affront to one's authority and a threat to one's classroom control.

Simply put, the questioning of rules, authority and the status quo doesn't exactly fit well with traditional education's long-standing image of well-behaved children following the rules in an orderly, well-run early childhood classroom. However, striving for this latter "ideal" often results in educators squelching children's exuberant questioning and resorting to "end-of-discussion"-type answers.

"Wonder is the beginning of wisdom."

SOCRATES

The problem with saying "no" all the time

Even before young children start questioning the world around them by using words and sentences, they do so by exploring. If a child is toddling toward danger, there's clearly a compelling reason to react with a decisive "NO!" with no further explanation needed (at least not in the moment). In instances such as when a toddler questions what would happen if she were to stick something in an uncovered outlet, you can appreciate her inquisitive nature while also ensuring she doesn't learn the answer from firsthand experience. (Of course, for safety's sake, all electrical outlets should always be appropriately covered.) But in instances where an answer or rule isn't so clear-cut, take the time to consider whether you need to discourage children's inquisitiveness and exploration. Ask yourself if it's simply a knee-jerk response you can work to control, so that you can better encourage children's curiosity and foster their WHY Skills.

Giving default answers such as "Because I said so" and frequently saying "no," especially without a specific reason, can undermine important WHY Skill development. It can be very tempting to use responses such as the following when faced with persistent questioning:

- "Because I said so."
- "No!" (reflexively and on repeat)
- "Just do as I say."
- "Follow the rules."
- "Stop asking so many questions."

Sure, it's easy to revere successful adults such as Steve Jobs and others who built their renown on their predilection for not just questioning the rules, but routinely breaking, disregarding and rewriting them. But when we're talking about young children, it is our role as early educators to make sure they understand the rules and learn how to follow them, especially when said rules are in place for good reason (such as for their health or safety). In this way, we also help them learn to play well with others and master important ME Skills. At the same time, your ultimate goal should be to make sure that as they grow up, children retain their ability as "Master Questioners"[53] to constructively and inquisitively question the world around them.

This admittedly poses a challenge: teach and enforce rules, or encourage children to disregard them? Punish children who continually question you and the way things are done, or praise them? Practically speaking, achieving a safe and healthy balance while effectively fostering WHY Skills is entirely possible if you understand how it fits with supporting appropriate child development.

DEVELOPMENTAL MILESTONES
Starting with WHY

WHY Skills are one of the categories of QI Skills that have less clearly defined milestones, which makes them less conducive to being presented in a neat, age-specific list. That said, it is nevertheless possible to generally describe how, where and when these skills fit into a child's growth and development.

Milestones

The first year

Even before young children are able to verbally demonstrate their WHY abilities, it is apparent that babies are intensely curious knowledge-seekers by nature. Their inquisitiveness and WHY-like search for answers start when they're very young, even during infancy. Long before they utter their first "why," babies and toddlers achieve a whole host of developmental milestones that represent early WHY Skills in the making.

They develop unspoken questions about how the world works, and get their answers by initially observing their adult caregivers before moving on to poking, prodding, testing, and even mouthing the things they're interested in. By nine months, most are developmentally able to start using their fingers to point at things, as a handy precursor to asking, "What's that?" Although infants' lack of language skills may keep them from forming well-worded questions, you can rest assured that they are nonetheless intensely curious and paying careful attention to what you say and do.

Toddlerhood

Beginning around age one and continuing throughout toddlerhood, children start learning words, naming familiar objects, and further exploring how these objects work for themselves. As an early educator, you play an important role in regularly supplying them with a wide range of objects and an abundance of answers to their "identification" questions.

Being well-versed in the value of knowing the names of things, pretty much every early educator I've ever met is happy to contribute to increasing young children's vocabulary and helping them gain a basic grasp of the world around them. Early on, toddlers' questions are likely to be relatively straightforward, so it's easy to entertain their curiosity. Of course, as they learn to stand and toddle on their own two feet, their curiosity about their world stands to keep everyone else on their toes!

Of note, the age at which children's cause-and-effect wheels really start turning also tends to signal the start of what is often referred to as the "age of independence," or, in some cases, the so-called "terrible twos." Think about it from their perspective: you think you know how the world works, only to discover it doesn't actually work that way. You get frustrated that you can't yet figure it out, and you lack the verbal ability to ask specific questions and understand the answers. If you dealt with this frustration on a daily basis, you might just throw a fit as well!

Preschoolers

It is with preschoolers that the WHY Skill milestones really take center stage. Children make a fairly obvious leap from being toddlers posing their very first rudimentary queries to three-, four- and five-year-olds who come to understand cause and effect, believe there is (or should be) a reason for almost everything, and who consequently challenge you with questions of all kinds. This is, after all, the period of time during which young children really start to develop the brain power (and the underlying executive function skills) needed to make logical connections between things.

These sorts of cognitive leaps enable children to begin to both ask and understand why and how things happen. As a result, their innate inquisitiveness and curiosity predictably present themselves in full force in the form of lots and lots of questions (one study found that children ask an average of 25 questions per hour!).[54] Young children want more and more information, and their developing WHY Skills (especially when partnered with their WILL, WIGGLE and WOBBLE Skills, all of which we'll soon be discussing) serve as their chief means of getting it.

Ultimately, you are responsible for striking a Goldilocks-like "not too much, not too little" balance between making sure children develop a healthy respect for the way things are and know how to follow rules on the one hand, and never giving up on questioning you, the rules, and the world around them on the other.

STAGE	WHY MILESTONES
0–2 months	unspoken questions, lots of observations
2–6 months	reach, grab, mouth, repeat
9 months	poking, prodding, and the addition of pointing
1–2 years	naming, exploring, basic questioning
3–5 years	increased frequency and complexity of questioning, enhanced vocabulary and understanding of cause and effect

CLASSROOM QI-NNECTIONS
Questioning, our role as educators

So there you have it: you play a key role, right alongside their parents, in giving children the opportunity to act on, retain and develop their WHY abilities. While it may be only natural for young children to be curious and question the world around them, what happens next during their formative early years is, in large part, going to be up to the approach taken by you and the other adults in their lives. After all, learning to put one's WHY Skills to work in a positive way takes not only understanding and patience, but also plenty of opportunity, support and encouragement. In the spirit of getting you off to a good start, the following are some approaches you can take to engage young children's inquiring minds.

Activities
- **Put into practice the mantra "there's no such thing as a stupid question."** Show through your words and actions that you actually believe this. Sure, some questions will inevitably be ill-timed, repetitive, or more appropriately handled by their parents, but given that young children ask questions as a primary method of understanding and engaging with the world, these should be encouraged rather than ridiculed.

A QUICK SNAPSHOT OF
THE POWER OF WHY

As the story goes, the inspiration for the invention of the Polaroid camera came in 1943 when the company's founder, Dr. Edwin Land, was asked by his three-year-old daughter to see the photo he snapped of her while on a family trip. After explaining to her the lengthy photo-developing process required, she reportedly asked the simple question, "Why can't I see the photos instantly?" The rest is history.[55,56]

- **Ask questions of your own.** Thoughtful questioning is a skill you want children to come to see as lifelong. Well before they're old enough to ask "Why?" for themselves, model for them how it's done by making a point to let them see you as someone who, as a lifelong learner, is always inquiring, wondering, and engaged in figuring out how the world works.

- **Answer unasked questions**. Even with young infants, it helps to remember that talking is teaching. Given just how early the foundation for WHY Skills begins to take shape, don't wait until the day children start asking you questions to recognize that they see the world as one big question mark. Rather, assume they'll be interested in just about whatever you have to say (especially if you are warm and engaging when you say it), and make it a habit to have fun narrating what's going on in the world around you. Point out and interact with things of interest, name them, and share your thoughts and insights as you go about your day together.

- **Praise questions, not just answers.** The more you respond to and appreciate a child's curiosity and questions, the more likely they are to continue asking them. This can be as easy as saying something like, "What an interesting question," or making clear that an inquiry is important by setting aside any distractions and giving your young inquisitor your full attention as you attempt to help them get their questions answered.

....

IT'S GOOD TO WONDER WHY

"It's what you bring to the children every day—
your listening, your caring, your enthusiasm,
and your responding to their ideas, thoughts, and
feelings—that encourages and inspires children
to ask questions. By responding thoughtfully to
children's questions . . . you're encouraging their
curiosity. Even when you don't know the answer, you're
letting them know it's good to wonder and ask."[57]

FRED ROGERS

....

- **Create an "ask-it basket."** As children get older and ask more detailed, frequent, and thought-provoking questions, consider creating a classroom "ask-it basket." I was first introduced to this idea during a webinar hosted by Gregg Behr and Ryan Rydzewski, the authors of *When You Wonder, You're Learning: Mister Rogers' Enduring Lessons for Raising Creative, Curious, Caring Kids*, who shared it as one they had gotten from a classroom teacher. The teacher would take the time to write down questions she wasn't in a position to answer at that moment (presumably because she either didn't know the answer, or didn't have the time to stop and address them) and put them in the basket to save for later. By simply declaring a child's question worthy of being written down and put in the ask-it-basket, you can reinforce that you are encouraging children's curiosity while also being able to pick a better time to address their questions. Consider engaging children's imagination, ideas, and artistic flair to turn a basket, cardboard box, or other container into a place where, with your help, they can have their important questions validated and answered at a time that's best for you and your class.

- **Increase your Q/A ratio**. Given all we've discussed about the importance of asking good questions versus simply having static answers, it stands to reason that our questions should eventually outnumber our answers. The Q/A ratio represents the number of questions asked relative to the number of answers given.[58] As early educators, young children rely on you for answers. Admittedly, it's nice to be seen as all-knowing (even if only in the eyes of a toddler), but it's also important to realize that helping children learn to make their way in the world today involves a balance between sharing your knowledge and helping them learn how to find their own answers.

- **Teach WHY manners**. Acknowledging the challenge of having even one, much less lots of children asking lots of questions isn't simply a matter of overlooking the inherent value of WHY Skills. More often than not, it has a whole lot to do with when, where and how (as well as which) questions are asked. Interrupting, not taking time to listen to the answer, or asking questions at inopportune times all run the risk of disrupting your flow or planned classroom activities. Such behaviors also tend to describe the tendencies of young children to a T. As you encourage children to keep asking questions, be sure to appreciate any efforts they make at engaging their ME and WE Skills of impulse control and awareness of others when, for example, they take turns, raise their hands, listen attentively to others, and refrain from interrupting (skills that can take quite some time to master). Also consider setting aside some time daily when children can ask questions to their heart's content and you can better appreciate their indefatigable questioning abilities—whether during free time or mealtime, or even at a specially designated "WHY time."

TAKING THE JOB OF "MASTER QUESTIONER" SERIOUSLY

One of the most helpful attitudes I've found when it comes to the early cultivation of WHY Skills is to consider it a child's job to ask lots of questions and (in short order) to question rules and limits, while also recognizing that it's your job to actually set some. Starting with eating, sleeping, peeing, pooping and playing, the fact of the matter is that babies and young children have only a few fundamentally important jobs to do. Questioning everything in the world around them—including you—is among the most important.

Having this awareness and being understanding can change your classroom expectations, as well as the way you respond to all of the many questions young children will inevitably ask of you. At the end of the day, it's much easier to appreciate and harder to get irritated by children's persistent questioning when you recognize that they are simply doing their job and constructing the foundation

of their WHY Skills. As it is also your job to set some limits, keep in mind that the rules you set and the answers
you give should be well thought out and serve a purpose
beyond simply exerting authority.

• **Beware of discouraging questions**. It's worth considering
when, why and how we typically discourage questioning
in our role as early educators. We have our reasons: we
have an agenda, we're short on time and have a lot to
get done, we don't know the answer, or we interpret
children's questioning as an affront to our professional
authority. Whatever the circumstance, these all represent
potential obstacles to children's WHY Skills development, so you'll want to make sure to balance the needs of
your classroom with encouraging their natural curiosity.

DISCOURAGING QUESTIONS

Given that the ability to ask good questions is just as valuable in adulthood as in early childhood, it's worth noting
cautionary research which suggests that the two biggest
inhibitors of adults being willing to ask questions are
(1) not wanting to look stupid, and (2) not wanting to be
viewed as uncooperative or disagreeable.[59]

• **Turn to books**. Reading books to young children can be an
easy and fun way to promote just about all the QI Skills.
With respect to WHY, books offer endless opportunities

to expose children to new ideas, pictures, and concepts that expand their worldview and understanding of how things work. To encourage questioning, allow time, at least in some of your read-aloud sessions, for children to take turns pointing at pictures, asking questions, and flipping back and forth to particularly intriguing pages or pictures rather than simply focusing on reading straight through from start to finish. Also feel free to toss in an occasional thought-provoking question of your own, starting with the simple find- or name-the-object variety, but eventually moving beyond those to questions for which you don't already know the answer. Just be sure that your questions enhance children's engagement and understanding, rather than inadvertently serve as a distraction or disruption as they work to focus on the story at hand.

- **Ask questions to which you don't know the answer.** Think about how many of the questions you ask of children over the course of the day are ones to which you already know the answer. While these types of questions can be quick and easy and can be used to reinforce concepts you've been introducing, they do far less to pique children's curiosity than asking more thought-provoking, open-ended questions that prompt further thought.

QI TAKEAWAYS: WHY

- WHY Skills involve asking not just "Why?" but all sorts of questions to better figure out how the world works.

- WHY Skills don't just involve the literal asking of questions: they also represent a mindset or a way of approaching the world that revolves around curiosity, wonder and inquisitiveness.

- Children are born curious and naturally ask lots of questions. This means that rather than just focusing on how best to *teach* WHY Skills, what's often needed is to simply make sure children have plenty of opportunities to ask questions and are encouraged to explore their world in this way.

QI REFLECTIONS: WHY

- Think about and make a list of ways you can encourage questioning in your classroom. Then, give the same attention to ways in which you might be discouraging children's questioning, curiosity and inquisitiveness (whether purposefully or inadvertently). How could you do more of the former and less of the latter?

- Think about how often students ask you questions over the course of the day. For those who aren't yet fully verbal, see if you can identify other ways in which they express their curiosity. For verbal children, consider how often you make time for their questions. How do you respond? Do their questions feel more like an interruption, or a fun and welcomed part of your teaching process?

- When a child asks you a question to which you don't know the answer, how do you respond? How might you model curiosity, show them ways to find answers to their questions, and further build their WHY Skills?

WILL
Self-Motivation and the Power of WILL

. . . .

"We do not need magic to change the world, we carry all the power we need inside ourselves already."[60]

J.K. ROWLING

"You have brains in your head. You have feet in your shoes. You can steer yourself any direction you choose."

DR. SEUSS

Oh, the Places You'll Go

I N 1930, newly minted Stanford psychologist Harry Harlow, recognizing that human and monkey minds are of similar complexity and development, set up a lab at the University of Wisconsin with a bunch of rhesus monkeys. Over the ensuing decades, he would go on to make breakthroughs in our understanding of infant attachment, human social behavior, learning and developmental psychology. Harlow and his colleagues conducted landmark studies that, to this day, inform our understanding of how the very QI Skills I've been describing develop—from the

WE Skills we've already covered, to the WILL Skills that we'll be exploring in this chapter.

Motivation and monkey business

Our pursuit of WILL begins with a relatively straightforward study in which Harlow gave his monkeys a contraption that required three distinct steps to open, and then observed whether they were able to figure it out. The results were simple enough, as the monkeys all learned how to operate the contraptions quickly and easily. What was more notable, however, was that each monkey did so independently, without any urging, instruction or rewards from the researchers. Problem solved? Well, yes and no.

This observed "monkeying around" with puzzles might not seem terribly surprising, until you consider the prevailing beliefs of the time. As renowned motivation expert Daniel Pink recounts in his *New York Times* best-selling book *Drive: The Surprising Truth About What Motivates Us*, scientists of Harlow's era believed there were only two main drivers of behavior[61]—those that were either:

1 biological in nature, namely satisfying hunger, thirst or sexual appetite, or

2 based on rewards and punishments.

Neither of these two standard drivers of behavior explained why Harlow's monkeys mastered the task at hand. After all, no rewards had been given (which, in monkey experiments, typically involve food or affection). Making the results all the more puzzling was the fact that, when subsequently offered rewards, the monkeys' performance actually got worse, not better.

As you might imagine, Harlow and his colleagues were left scratching their heads, wondering what exactly the driving force was behind the monkeys' seemingly purpose-driven behavior. The answer is what our next QI Skill is all about: WILL.

> 🔼 **WILL Skills** relate to motivation and drive, but more specifically involve *intrinsic* motivation and the skills of self-motivation, dedication and drive, commitment, conscientiousness and persistence.

What is WILL?

When my three children entered kindergarten, each was officially inducted into an all-inclusive club their elementary school principal aptly dubbed "The Can-Do Club." The club focused on recognizing its young members for their hard work, effort and follow-through. That same can-do spirit goes a long way toward defining the essence of WILL Skills.

These skills comprise all of the highly valued, get-the-job-done, go-getter attributes that help us persevere, overcome adversity and thrive in life, including:

- Commitment
- Conscientiousness
- Determination
- Drive
- Gumption
- Persistence

Of note, WILL Skills require attention, focus, and self-control, making them highly dependent on ME Skills and their underlying executive function skills. In a way, WILL Skills are ME Skills put into action, with motivation at the heart of it all.

The important thing to know right off the bat is that there are actually two types of motivation. The first is *extrinsic* motivation, which involves performing an action or behavior to receive a reward or avoid punishment. But the kind of motivation that we're talking about in the context of WILL does not come in the form of a gold star, ice cream or M&Ms. The driving force behind all of the WILL Skills is the feeling of pride that comes with accomplishing a task.

"You can motivate by fear. And you can motivate by reward. But both of these are only temporary. The only lasting thing is self-motivation."[62]

HOMER RICE
former American football player and coach

Motivation from within

Going back to Harlow's monkeys, what Pink credits that experiment with bringing to light is the other, previously unrecognized and powerful driver of behavior that we now know as *intrinsic* motivation. This recognition of an inner force or "drive" (the latter term popularized by Pink) is captured in his summary description of Harlow's results: "The monkeys solved the puzzles simply because they found it gratifying to solve puzzles. They enjoyed it. The joy of [accomplishing] the task was its own reward."[63]

But it wouldn't be monkeys alone that would provide evidence of intrinsic motivation. To study this phenomenon in humans, psychology graduate student Edward Deci challenged university students with a different kind of puzzling task. As it turned out, his human subjects also showed the same "inherent tendencies to seek out novelty and challenges" and to "extend and exercise their capacities, to explore, and to learn."[64] As a result, intrinsic motivation was launched on its way to becoming recognized as a key aspect of human nature, while the offering of external rewards (in Deci's experiments, money replaced bananas) was coming to be recognized as potentially detrimental to the development of intrinsic motivation (not to mention the development of other key components of QI Skills, including creativity).

Setting our sights on WILL

You might be thinking that all of this is fairly straightforward. After all, what parent or educator doesn't want children to grow up self-motivated, and to help them become confident in setting and pursuing long-term goals and striving to achieve their personal best? But it's not always quite that easy.

For anyone committed to the strategic goal of fostering children's WILL abilities, it's worth first addressing a couple of common "inconsistencies" in how people often think about and approach aspects of WILL. The first is the prevailing attitude toward strong-willed children; the other has to do with M&Ms.

A word on being strong-willed

In light of what you've already learned about WILL in this chapter, being strong-willed surely must be a good thing, right? It's a trait that seems to fit perfectly into the adult world's view of determination, persistence, and all the other WILL Skill characteristics listed above. Yet when children are referred to as "strong-willed" the connotation is almost always negative, implying that they are troublesome, problematic, or difficult.

In principle, we may very much want children to have strong WILL Skills. Put into practice in the early years, however, it can sometimes prove to be a bit challenging.

Will pee for M&Ms

A common potty-training tactic of parents and early educators is to offer a reward for successfully using the potty. This could be a treat like M&Ms, or some other kind of reward. The effect of offering a tantalizing, extrinsic reward for the accomplishment of a task, whether being potty-trained, answering a question, or eating their broccoli, is the same We risk derailing young children's WILL Skill development by teaching them early and often to expect rewards for any and all jobs well done. Yes, in the short term this can help them complete a task for which they seem to require some extrinsic motivation. But if we don't step back to see how pervasive this practice is—incorporated by both parents and educators in ways that are more widespread than is often appreciated—we stand to undercut children's ability to connect with and respond to intrinsic motivation.

Avoiding the mitten trap

Even for those who are aware of just how common and potentially problematic the use of extrinsic rewards is in the classroom and in the lives of our youngest children, it's all too easy to unintentionally fall into the extrinsic reward trap.

One of my favorite activities at the 200-student educational childcare center I owned was our annual mitten drive. With the goal of helping young children learn about empathy and kindness through hands-on QI Skill experiences, we encouraged students to bring in mittens to donate to local families in need. Toddlers and preschoolers would dash up to me at the front desk, pull mittens from their pockets, and proudly proclaim, "I brought mittens!" Parents fully supported these efforts, recognizing the value of encouraging their children to think about others, do good, and actively develop their WE Skills. (The hands-on nature of the activity also involved WIGGLE Skills, which we will discuss in the next chapter.)

During this mitten drive month, teachers would get in the spirit as well, helping the preschoolers make tally marks to keep track of how many mittens each classroom collected. As the total number grew—one year reaching as high as 700 pairs—so did everyone's excitement. One day, a member of my well-intentioned management team asked me whether we could reward the classroom that brought in the most mittens with a pizza party. Caught up in the celebratory sentiment, I approved the idea. It was not until well after the fact that I realized I had just managed to turn an activity that successfully engendered intrinsic feelings of pride and accomplishment into one that promised extrinsic rewards. Instead of the pride associated with doing something nice for others, I had effectively shifted the reward from sharing mittens to eating pizza.

To be sure, as in my case, parents and early educators are often well-intentioned in making these sorts of decisions. But this shift of approach, especially repeated time and again, can have consequences. Children who are conditioned to perform for extrinsic rewards risk failing to develop the very same inner drive that is so valued later in life, especially when faced with challenging tasks. Just as important, if children grow up lacking intrinsic motivation, they miss experiencing the deep feelings of fulfillment and happiness that come from doing something well for its own sake—from sharing the warmth of mittens, to learning new things, to mastering tough challenges.

It's easy to rationalize the use of extrinsic rewards, especially during the most demanding early years. Anything that gets children to do what we want or need them to do understandably seems like a good thing. But, given what child development, business and social science all tell us about the potential for unintended consequences, we need to keep in mind that the cumulative effect of rewards can crack the foundation of young children's developing WILL Skills.

PUTTING WILL TO WORK: YOU KNOW IT WHEN YOU SEE IT

One of my favorite examples of WILL Skills in action is a short video clip of a preschooler attempting to build a tower of blocks—you know the kind, with the blocks stacked from big to small. From the outset, it's clear that the child's early tower-building attempts aren't going to work so well, as he starts by placing some of the smaller blocks on the bottom, leading to a shaky foundation and a predictable toppling of the tower. Add to this several children running by and inadvertently kicking or knocking over his blocks, and the young boy's dogged determination becomes increasingly impressive.

Through trial and error, patient persistence, and by maintaining his focus despite all the distractions around him, he finally and proudly completes his tower. Having seen this real-world video demonstration of WILL shown on more than one occasion to audiences consisting of high-level business executives, I can tell you that, without fail, someone always remarks, "Well, *that's* the kid you'd hire!"

While we can't always put our finger on, much less measure WILL, you know it when you see it. And everyone—parents, educators and business executives alike—knows they want it!

DEVELOPMENTAL MILESTONES
Putting WILL to the test

So what does WILL look like in young children? If you stop and think about it, early childhood is full of examples of WILL, because it serves as a driving force that enables children to try over and over and over again at every age and stage of development.

Take babies, for example. Over months and years they persist in cooing, babbling and imitating their way to the ultimate goal of not just talking, but being understood and able to effectively communicate. You also certainly see WILL in the "do-it-myself" determination of two-year-olds who attempt to dress themselves or insist on brushing their own teeth.

No discussion of WILL Skills would be complete without mention of the classic and inspirational children's book *The Little Engine That Could.*[65] From the Little Engine's "I think I can, I think I can, I think I can" to its associated feeling of accomplishment when belief becomes reality, this is the track we should hope all children learn to follow. It's worth noting, however, that in today's high-stakes world the

Little Engine could just as easily end up on a different, less self-motivated developmental track, depending on how parents and early educators alike approach our critical role.

A parenting cartoon shared with me many years ago, which is easily applicable to early educators as well, serves to capture this cautionary note particularly well. In the cartoon, a little engine sits idling, stuck at the base of a mountain. Rather than "I think I can," this little engine says, "Push me!...MOM!... Well? I'M WAITING!" The accompanying caption reads, "The little engine whose parents did everything for him."[66]

STAGE	WILL MILESTONES
0–12 months	rolling, reaching, babbling, imitating
1–2 years	toddling, self-feeding
2 years	do-it-myself determination
3–5 years	enhanced cognitive and motor skills allow for more opportunities to figure out, assemble, and achieve increasing independence

CLASSROOM QI-NNECTIONS
Where there's a WILL there's a way

Now for the good news: with a little WILL forethought, you can get away from the "if-then" transactional approach to motivating young children that is characterized by peeing for M&Ms. Having said that, though, I also feel the need to acknowledge that it's likely impossible (and unnecessary) to avoid rewards and punishments altogether. Resorting to handing out a gold star sticker or a sweet treat every now and then is not going to ruin all of the good WILL Skills you're working to build. The key, as with so many aspects of life, is moderation. If you commit to limiting how many times you employ rewards so that it doesn't become a recurring pattern, you should be able to avoid undermining your students' self-motivation, determination and can-do attitude.

By thinking through your long-term professional goals as an early educator, as well as the kind of "little engines" you want young children to grow up to be, you can start to be more intentional in building a strong foundation for their developing WILL Skills. When faced with the assertive or "willful" child, just remind yourself that, if cultivated in thoughtful and productive ways like those recommended below, the very same assertiveness and determination that can admittedly prove a tad bit challenging at age three will likely serve that child well at age 23.

While WILL Skills aren't technically something you teach, the following activities can help you recognize, support, nurture and engage children's self-motivation and establish a strong WILL Skill foundation.

Activities

- **Avoid engaging in "if-then."** Knowing all we now know about the long-term demotivating potential of (or dependency on) extrinsic rewards, consciously think about and limit your use of them for jobs well done. This doesn't mean don't celebrate: just be judicious and avoid making every task a conditional if-then-driven achievement. Instead, make children's self-motivation a cause for celebration in and of itself, and pride in their "work" the ultimate reward. To this end, simple, supportive affirmations—as simple as remembering to say "I'm so proud of your effort" or "You should be very proud of yourself"— go a long way.

- **Model self-motivated behavior.** One of the ways you can foster children's motivation is by being motivated yourself. In a practical sense, this may involve allowing your students to see or hear you talk about participating in activities or working hard on something simply because you enjoy the feeling of accomplishment, not just doing work or tasks for which you're rewarded.

- **Resist swooping in.** Remember, WILL involves *self*-motivation. It also involves stick-with-it-ness. This means that young children—even infants—need to be given the time and opportunity to try things for themselves. Whether it's a six-month-old reaching for, scooting toward or trying to roll to an out-of-reach toy, a nine-month-old trying to pull themselves to a stand, a two-year-old pulling up their own pants, or three- and four-year-olds insisting on doing everything "all by myself," make sure you appreciate the WILL that drives these behaviors. Resist the urge to take over, even when things get messy—like when toddlers insist on feeding themselves!

- **Anticipate an occasional battle of wills.** As young children develop minds of their own and increasingly apply their WILL Skills, it only stands to reason that this will occasionally lead to conflict. In fact, minor skirmishes are quite predictable when young children are motivated to do and get what they want and, at the same time, expected to share. A number of QI Skills apply here. Conflict of this sort often results simply because young children haven't yet mastered the ME (self-control) and WE (relationships, empathy) Skills necessary to adjust their competing WILL-minded behaviors. As you help children learn to navigate these situations, keep in mind that the same drive and determination that causes young children to refuse to stop what they're doing, wait their turn, or return another child's toy can ultimately be a contributor to their future success when they learn to apply it in a more prosocial and productive manner.

- **Prioritize perseverance.** Promote and praise age-appropriate stick-with-it-ness and persistence with challenging tasks. Let children know you appreciate when they help out with or complete monotonous or time-consuming tasks, such as putting away toys. Recognize that younger children have shorter attention spans, so what may seem like giving up in the context of an older child may actually represent an impressive effort for their age. For example, when a two-year-old keeps trying to build a tower of blocks for 15 minutes, that's WILL worth celebrating! At a certain point, of course, it's fine to let young children stop or to give them a hand, but you might just be surprised by how often they choose to keep trying, master a new challenge, and are rewarded with a positive feeling because they persisted when simply given the chance and some encouragement, as needed.

- **Present them with puzzles.** It's no coincidence that researchers often use puzzles to test intrinsic motivation, since the reward is the satisfaction that comes with completing them. Given the chance, even very young children can prove themselves to be good puzzle problem-solvers.

- **Take it slow.** What children really need to develop WILL, in addition to your support, is time. As you go about implementing your daily curriculum and classroom routines, consider whether you may be unintentionally sending children the message that you value what's quick and easy over putting in the effort, especially when that effort takes more time than you have allotted. Certainly, there will be times when you'll have to jump in to help speed up the process. But whenever possible, be sure to set aside the time necessary for children to work at mastering and eventually completing new and challenging tasks, as it will prove to be WILL time well spent.

- **Encourage practice.** Although it can sometimes feel dull or overly repetitive, practice is a great way for small children (and even adults) to put WILL Skills to good use. Besides learning to develop a new skill or talent and persist through challenges, you can make sure they learn to feel pride not only when their effort pays off, but also as a result of practicing routinely.

- **Make it a choice.** Giving young children choices and letting them feel like they have a say in what they're doing does a lot for enhancing their motivation to engage with and put the effort into tackling their chosen task.

- **Give them goals.** Take time to teach children about setting long-term goals, bearing in mind that next week or even tomorrow can count as "long term" for a young child. This could be as simple as encouraging them to complete a puzzle, learn to read, or play on a team. Start with reasonably easy-to-accomplish goals, but don't stop there: help children build up over time to the sorts of "stretch" goals that take more time, effort and perseverance.

- **Tap into their passions.** Pay attention to what drives your students or what they're most excited about doing. When babies are just learning to roll, for example, motivation can come in the form of a few words of encouragement and a toy placed just out of reach. Taking note of which activities (art, singing, reading, playing outside, computers) and topics (certain animals, trucks, superheroes) seem to spark the most interest for any given child can go a long way towards encouraging them to more WILL-fully engage. In the case of my toddler son (all the way through age eight or so), his passion was elephants—so much so that, even when he was quite young, he would listen attentively to stories, dress himself, and draw impressively well, so long as these activities in some way involved a pachyderm.

- **Play**. Play is certainly a hot topic in early childhood (and beyond), with significant emphasis being placed on the fact that play doesn't just support learning, it *is* learning. (We'll talk more about this as we explore in more detail how to put QI Skills into action through play later in the book.) It's worth noting that one of the key features routinely ascribed to play is the fact that it is, almost by definition, intrinsically motivating. Creating opportunities for plenty of playtime, as well as adding playful elements to topics and tasks you're hoping to teach, can be a fun and valuable way to engage young children and help them develop all of their QI Skills, including their WILL Skills.

QI TAKEAWAYS: WILL

- WILL Skills aren't really that hard to see: you'll know them when you see them, so long as you remember to look.

- Not all motivation is equal. While extrinsic motivation is driven by the promise of rewards (or threat of punishment), it is *intrinsic* motivation or self-motivation that defines the essence of WILL.

- Intrinsic motivation isn't something that is formally taught. Rather, as a key element of WILL, it is something that can be recognized, encouraged, supported and praised.

- Developing and encouraging WILL takes time—the time necessary to keep trying, practicing and figuring things out.

- Play is intrinsically motivating, which means there's almost always an element of WILL in play.

- WILL is reliant on and supports just about all of the other QI Skills.

QI REFLECTIONS: WILL

- Consider a typical day in your classroom. What might WILL look like in your students? Can you identify ways in which you support or allow children to practice their WILL Skills?

- Instead of just recognizing accomplishments, think instead about how you can highlight effort. What words do (or could) you use to spotlight WILL with the same sense of enthusiasm and pride? How easy or difficult do you find it to recognize WILL?

- Think about the children in your classroom. How can you tell when they're motivated? What do you typically need to do or say to keep them motivated? How often do you find yourself defaulting or feeling the need to offer rewards? Do you feel you give rewards more out of necessity, or out of habit?

- Think about the last time you were really motivated to accomplish something. What motivated you? What was it that kept you going? What challenges made it difficult to persevere and accomplish your goal?

WIGGLE
Putting WIGGLEs to Work
· ·

"Thinking is a full-body activity ... Thinking while
moving brings the full range of our faculties into play."
ANNIE MURPHY PAUL,
The Extended Mind: The Power of
Thinking Outside of the Body

AROUND THE TIME I first sat down to write about
WIGGLE Skills, I happened to catch a story on the
morning news about parents in a Florida town protest-
ing the elimination of recess in their local elementary school.
Sadly, this story wasn't the first (or last) of its kind: schools
struggling to meet rigorous national academic assessment
standards have long resorted to cutting recess as a way to
create more time for learning.

Further catching my attention, the very next feature story
happened to be about the growing popularity of walking
meetings and treadmill desks to help increase physical activity
at work. The reporter commented on how today's employers,
increasingly aware of how beneficial getting up and moving can be to both overall health and to the productivity of
their workforces, were implementing practical solutions to
encourage these sorts of beneficial get-up-and-get-moving

behaviors. The focus of these two juxtaposed stories wasn't exactly breaking news. In fact, the idea began to enter our national consciousness at least a decade ago, as evidenced by prominent Silicon Valley–based business innovator Nilofer Merchant's TED Talk "Got a Meeting? Take a Walk," which has garnered nearly four million views to date.[67] That was followed shortly thereafter by Merchant's *Harvard Business Review* blog post, in which she ominously but astutely declared that "Sitting is the smoking of our generation."[68]

Despite the call for more activity, schools still seem to be operating largely under the premise that what's most important in an academic setting is for students to be stationary. The concept of "seat time," a system that designates the amount of (often mandated) time students are required to spend in school, has long been embedded in traditional education. The not-so-subtle implication of this concept is that students must be in their seats and sitting still in order to learn. To return to those back-to-back news stories, you have to admit that there's a pretty striking disconnect between eliminating physical activity from children's curricula while simultaneously trying to incorporate it back into the working world for adults.

As it is not that far removed from elementary education, it occurred to me it was high time we take a closer look at what early education is and is not doing during the earliest years to encourage young children to get moving. This isn't just for the sake of improving their health and well-being, but also as a way of actually enhancing their learning. This is what our fifth QI Skill, WIGGLE, is all about: embodied learning and children's innate propensity to move, interact and play as a fun, effective, hands-on way to explore and learn about their world.

What's in a WIGGLE?

In one sense, WIGGLE Skills describe exactly what the verb "wiggle" suggests: the physical act of moving, being active, and generally being in constant motion. But while these are certainly essential elements of WIGGLE, they represent only part of the picture. Key to understanding the concept of WIGGLE is recognizing that WIGGLE actually spans both physical and intellectual restlessness, and that these two go hand in hand. Children's ability to move around and explore their world from day one is essential not only for their physical health and development but also for their cognitive development, as it enhances their engagement in active learning and their ability to put their natural-born inquisitiveness (WHY Skills) into action.

We know that a core principle of early childhood is that children learn through play. From the time they are infants through toddlerhood and beyond, much of that playing is associated with a whole lot of motion: shaking rattles, stacking blocks and knocking them down, picking up toys, rolling balls, opening and closing drawers, crawling, cruising, climbing, pulling up, and engaging in countless other activities that actively put the world to the test and seldom involve sitting still. When given the opportunity, children quite literally WIGGLE their way through childhood—and that's a good thing.

PLAY: "THE HIGHEST FORM OF RESEARCH"

In addition to his renowned theories on light, motion, and relativity, Einstein is credited with recognizing that "play is the highest form of research." While this is true for many reasons, the fact that play so often involves physical activity and movement certainly factors into it, as it has been shown that information learned while moving is better remembered.

Young children are expert hands-on researchers, so your job as an early educator is to provide them with plentiful opportunities to move and engage with the game or subject at hand, rather than just to tame or suppress their innate WIGGLE tendencies. This may require you to shift your thinking a bit about the constant motion and restlessness characteristic of early childhood so that you come to see (and help direct and shape) it as a lifelong WIGGLE Skill to be appreciated, encouraged, cultivated and positively directed.

So what's in a WIGGLE? Although WIGGLE is admittedly harder to pin down and divide into specific subsets of skills, it involves:

- Hands-on exploration
- Agility
- Movers and shakers
- Taking action
- Physical and intellectual restlessness

§ **WIGGLE Skills** are the skills put into action through embodied learning, based on the understanding that physical and intellectual restlessness go hand in hand. These skills recognize that hands-on interaction with and physical exploration of the world around us results in enhanced engagement and learning.

How the world views WIGGLE

If the idea of learning and motion going hand-in-hand seems a bit abstract, take a moment to think about how often we use action words in the adult world to describe ideas, goals and cognitive abilities. We appreciate those who cognitively take baby *steps* or big *leaps* forward as *moving* in the right direction; we recognize the need to allow for *wiggle* room, in both a conceptual and a physical sense; we admire people for their *hustle*; and we *actively* encourage setting *stretch* goals and *reaching* for the stars. We recognize *movers and shakers* as people who get the job done; place high value on *agility* (the ability to *move quickly* and easily); and cheer on those who *take action* and are *active* participants.

In short, if the way we talk about both physical and intellectual restlessness is any indication—which I would suggest to you it is—the perpetual motion associated with WIGGLE is clearly of value in today's world. And yet as Annie Murphy Paul, author of *The Extended Mind*, astutely points out, we nevertheless tend to act as if there's something virtuous about controlling the impulse to move, associating stillness with steadiness, seriousness and industriousness, and fidgeting with "a certain moral shiftiness."[69]

....

"Our culture conditions us to see mind and body
as separate—and so we separate, in turn, our
periods of thinking from our bouts of exercise . . .
[and yet] research shows that kids return from a session
on the playground better able to focus their attention
and to engage their executive function faculties."[70]

ANNIE MURPHY PAUL

....

The mind-movement connections

Philosopher Henry David Thoreau has been credited with making the "mind-movement" connection that helps to define WIGGLE Skills back in the 19th century, noting (in true-to-19th-century prose), "Methinks that the moment my legs begin to move, my thoughts begin to flow."[71] In the 1960s, researchers started to more concretely establish this connection between physical activity and performance on cognitive tasks. Since the 1990s, researchers have been providing ever more support for the belief that being physically active doesn't just improve our physical health, but also boosts our ability to think more clearly and creatively. A Stanford University study, for example, found that simply walking was sufficient to heighten creative inspiration by an average of about 60%,[72] while using a standing desk rather than sitting has been shown to enhance executive functioning in elementary school students.[73]

Meanwhile, Harvard psychiatrist and researcher John Ratey, best known for his efforts to advance the mind-movement connection, put forth a best-selling book's worth of WIGGLE-relevant findings suggesting that physical activity inherently prepares learners by conferring a whole host of benefits extending well beyond just physical health and well-being. These include improved impulse control, behavior, attention (ME Skills), motivation (WILL Skills), mood, anxiety regulation and self-esteem.

While our understanding of exactly how physical activity bolsters brainpower has undoubtedly increased significantly since back when Thoreau was "methinking," it continues to be a subject of significant interest and inquiry. Researchers in Switzerland, for example, published a study in the journal *Brain Plasticity* which found that mice who ran on wheels developed twice the normal number of new neurons and showed improved abilities on cognitive tests afterward.[74] Other studies have found that stepping away from your computer mouse to move your body, such as going for a walk, replenishes your energy, which in turn improves your focus, concentration, creativity and productivity when you return to work.[75]

"Creative thinkers try new things and move with the changing world."

ELAINE DUNDON

The Seeds of Innovation: Cultivating the Synergy That Fosters New Ideas

Although the body of research explaining this complex body-brain connection is not yet fully developed, what is clear is that physically engaging in hands-on exploration rather than rigidly enforcing seat time is an effective way to actively enhance learning. Allowing children to develop their WIGGLE Skills starting in their earliest years is increasingly being understood as essential for cultivating the valuable lifelong habit of using our bodies to move, learn, explore and discover.

WIGGLE WHILE YOU WORK:
INDUSTRY'S EMBRACE OF MOVEMENT

Applications of the mind-movement findings that define WIGGLE aren't just confined to the classroom. Several have made their way into today's business world as a means of sparking innovation, as evidenced by WIGGLE activities such as walking meetings and treadmill desks.

Taking a page from the early childhood playbook, I always enjoy walking into a meeting or conference to find a handful of small, colorful toys or objects strategically placed on the table so that adult attendees can toss, stack, fiddle, fidget, and otherwise play with them. These manipulatives are not set out simply for entertainment or distraction (or in honor of "bring your child to work" day), but as an intentional effort to keep attendees engaged by allowing their bodies to keep moving, offering hands-on opportunities to interact and thus keep everyone's creative juices actively flowing.

In *The Innovator's DNA: Mastering the Five Skills of Disruptive Innovators*, Harvard Business School professor Clayton Christensen notes that innovators rarely sit still: what just about all of them have in common is that they're constantly out investigating the world around them.[76] In other words, for anyone in the business of early childhood, there's a moving argument to be made that the recognition of WIGGLE Skills and the benefits of moving around in the world applies as much to innovators, the business world, and adults in general as it does to infants and young children in your classrooms!

A "wiggle" by any other name

As we focus on WIGGLE in the classroom, I want you to consider for a moment the language commonly used to describe active young children: "fidgety," "antsy," "restless." As I was pulling together this list, I was also introduced to the word *shpilkes*, which apparently does a similarly good job of conveying (in Yiddish) how those of us responsible for keeping up with young children typically view their impulses to move and explore, touch new things, and test out all sorts of ways of interacting with the world around them. *Shpilkes* literally (or at least in a "see also" sense) means "ants in the pants," or the inability to sit still. Most of the time, it's an expression bursting with nervous energy: "Can't you sit still for even a second? You've got the *shpilkes!*" an adult might admonish a young child. No surprise, the alternate definitions of *shpilkes* as "impatience" or "agitation" have similarly negative connotations.

In contrast to the 21st-century adult world's embrace of WIGGLE Skills, young children's tendency to be in constant motion is all too often viewed in the early childhood classroom as something that needs to be limited, controlled or contained, with early educators and parents alike accepting the picture of a "well-behaved child" as one who is calm, quiet, sits still, and doesn't reach, touch, grab, poke, or otherwise "get into" things. This outdated image does nothing to help us learn to truly embrace active play and hands-on exploration—with all the noise and energy and motion that tends to come with it—as important work for three-year-olds. Instead, the culture of early childhood runs the risk of mistakenly accepting the definition of "work" as synonymous with "seat work," and at best treating any sparks of restless energy as something we need to extinguish, sort of like removing the batteries from an Energizer Bunny.

Given these attitudes toward WIGGLE, it's not all that surprising that the mindsets of even well-intentioned early educators can play out in the classroom in ways that work against the early development of children's WIGGLE Skills.

WIGGLE restrictions

So what stands in the way of our children's earliest WIGGLE development, aside from generally dismissive attitudes toward it? One of the most pervasive WIGGLE-prohibitive practices young children face is what I have long referred to as the "strapped-in" mentality. Just think of all the many items designed and used on a daily basis during children's earliest years expressly to keep them buckled down and restrained: car seats, strollers, bouncy seats, stationary activity centers, baby carriers, swings, highchairs and booster seats are but a few examples.

As a pediatrician mom who juggled three kids very close in age, as well as operating a 200-student educational childcare center, I am in no way discounting the fact that each of these items can serve a very useful purpose. They can ensure a child's safety, as well as helping with soothing, feeding, play and transport. I'll also be the first to acknowledge that I couldn't have survived the early years without them.

However, when we become overly reliant on shifting babies and young children from one strapped-in device to another, we give them little opportunity to roll, scoot or crawl. Toddlers run the risk of being left with no time to toddle (or WOBBLE). All too often preschoolers—even if only figuratively restrained—aren't afforded the time they need to actively engage in play and learning. In other words, adopting this "safe-and-secure," strapped-in approach stands to significantly limit children's opportunities to work on their WIGGLE Skills, as well as all of their other QI Skills. Not to mention that this strapped-in approach limiting movement can impact a child's future physical fitness and well-being.

IT'S ABOUT TIME TO WIGGLE

A University of Washington study involving preschoolers found that active play constituted a mere 12% of the young study subjects' day, with the children playing outside an average of barely 30 minutes per day. Napping accounted for nearly a third of the preschoolers' time, with the rest of their day spent eating or otherwise engaged in sedentary activities.[77]

Sit still and listen

Several years back, a new mom of an eight-month-old mentioned to me how excited she felt that her baby was no longer just interested in trying to chew on books whenever she attempted to read to him: he was starting to sit in her lap and look at the pages while she read. She could even get through several baby books at a time. As someone who's always been passionate about reading aloud with young children, I could absolutely understand her excitement.

However, her comment also jogged something else I have long felt worthwhile for all early educators to ask ourselves: Why is it that reading to young children in an early childhood classroom must always be a stationary activity? Why, based on all we know about WIGGLE and embodied learning, do we picture an eager and engaged child, one who is truly ready to learn, as a child who sits perfectly still, "crisscross applesauce," in their designated spot on a reading rug? As one who doesn't fidget, move, or otherwise WIGGLE while listening to stories? Or, for that matter, as one who keeps books out of their mouth? Sure, it may feel nothing short of unnatural to allow children to more actively engage, but when you take a moment to think about how beneficial it is for young children to WIGGLE, holding on to this belief that children need to be perfectly still in order to be read to can be counterproductive.

As someone trained in the developmental milestones of early literacy, I'd even go so far as to suggest that handling and chewing on books represent some of the earliest WIGGLE precursors of literacy. To become proficient in a skill, children must first be interested, curious and engaged, and for infants, nothing says engaged more than when they use the tools they have available (i.e., their hands and mouths) for exploring. When viewed in this light, gumming the corners of a book as a first (albeit wet and slobbery) step towards literacy doesn't seem so outrageous. From there, toddlers learn to hold the book and turn the pages; then they discover there are words on those pages; and before long they realize the pages they've been handling contain the stories they've been hearing, and that one day they will be able to read themselves. Fortunately, someone got smart and created durable board books, so that we all can and should feel comfortable allowing even gumming-prone babies to handle and explore books in the WIGGLE ways that come so naturally to them.

PRESENTING THE BOARD BOOK!

According to the curator of the Baldwin Library of Historical Children's Literature at the University of Florida, contemporary board books date back to the 1930s, when they were made of very thick cardboard that could be bitten (or thrown) with little to no damage. This was a pretty big deal, if you consider the fact that throughout most of the 18th and 19th centuries, books primarily delivered tales of religion and morality rather than entertainment. They were considerably more valuable (and thus expensive) than today's durable little board books—so expensive that young children would never have been allowed to handle, much less encouraged to bite or gum them.[78,79]

When my children were young, I read literally hundreds of books to them each year—but that by no means implies they sat perfectly motionless on my lap as we turned page after page. Rather, I would often read while they played, crawled, colored or otherwise WIGGLED attentively nearby—quiet activities that helped keep them engaged with the stories much longer than they would have otherwise. They would stop what they were doing to eagerly turn their attention to take in the illustrations or turn the pages; in some instances, they would even draw pictures related to the stories we were reading. Through these and other signs, I knew that they were absorbing the vocabulary and stories in the books, not to mention enjoying the shared activity of reading at least as much, but most likely a whole lot more, than if they had been sitting perfectly still. Lending yet more support to this tried-and-true hands-on approach to reading aloud, recent research tells us that the effort required to sit still places competing demands on the very same region of the brain—the prefrontal cortex, home of the executive function skills—that must be engaged to pay attention to what's being read.

A MOVING STORY ABOUT READING ALOUD

By the ages of five and six, my two oldest children were so enthusiastic about listening to stories read aloud that they would sit and attentively listen to chapter books written for children several years older. One book in particular, naturalist author Jean Craighead George's *Julie of the Wolves*, so captured their attention with its story of a girl who gets lost on the Arctic tundra and slowly figures out how to become accepted into a wolf pack to survive, that I ended up reading the entire three-book series aloud to them—twice.

My initial concerns that these books, written at a fifth-grade reading level, might be a bit over my children's heads proved to not be warranted. For my youngest, however, I had no such concerns to begin with, if only because he was not yet three and had never really sat still long enough to convince me he was listening. He would wander his way in and around whatever room we were reading in, always moving but staying in my line of sight as he contentedly entertained and played by himself while showing no signs of following along with the story. But, as it turned out, he was listening all along—so much so that pretty much every stuffed animal he subsequently ever owned was named "Amoraq" (the leader of the wolf pack that "adopted" Julie in the story) and went on to read (and re-read multiple times) the series himself. To this day, even in his 20s, the wolf remains his favorite animal.

DEVELOPMENTAL MILESTONES
Let's WIGGLE!

As we've discussed, even before they're born babies WIGGLE in utero. Infants WIGGLE as they discover their hands and feet. Toddlers WIGGLE all day long—and that's just the beginning. Below are some of the key motor and cognitive milestones that allow young children to more actively and physically engage in the world.

Milestones

Newborn

Born with a whole host of involuntary reflexes, newborns have little intentional control over anything more than basic movements. That said, some can lift their head a bit to take a look around, and it's only a short time before their increasing muscle strength will allow them to move more. Even at birth they're capable of "worming" their way up to their mother's breast and sticking out their tongue (the so-called tongue-thrust reflex) to breastfeed or bottle feed.

Two months

Although still not demonstrating too many outward signs of constant motion, two-month-olds can typically hold up their heads and start pushing up when lying on their tummy. Movements of their arms and legs at this age become smoother and more controlled as babies gain some control over involuntary reflexes. This also includes starting to open their hands—a meaningful step towards being able to intentionally use them to explore. While not all that mobile themselves, two-month-olds start looking intently at toys that in only a few short months they'll be able to reach out and grab, and spend time preparing themselves for what's to come by watching and learning from you as you move around.

Four months

Babies at this age begin taking even more control of their movements, holding their heads up high and steady without support and pushing up onto their elbows and forearms when lying on their stomach—movements that afford them a new and improved view of the world they will soon be able to more actively explore. As notable first steps towards both the cognitive and physical mastery of hands-on exploration, four-month-olds look at their hands with interest, bring their hands to their mouths (which, of course, is one of the main ways babies first start to explore the world), are able to hold on to toys put in their hands, and may even take a swing at nearby toys.

Six months

Six-month-olds start to demonstrate their curiosity about things in an even more physical way: they make an effort to reach for objects of interest and make a habit of exploring things by putting them in their mouths. While still not all that mobile, their budding ability to push up and roll from their tummy to their back and to start to sit up with a little support suggests that a more active age of exploration is rapidly approaching.

Nine months

The ability to get to a sitting position independently and remain there without support offers up a whole new world-view for nine-month-olds. This allows them to watch and then look for the objects dropped out of sight that they will soon be attempting to go get for themselves. They are now able to move things back and forth between hands, as well as more intentionally use their fingers to "rake" food and other objects towards themselves.

Figuring out and then amusing themselves by banging two objects together serves as both a cognitive and a movement milestone at this age. While, technically speaking, crawling isn't considered an official milestone, it's not uncommon to see an occasional baby at this age put their hands and knees to the ground and start crawling in all sorts of quirky and creative ways. As for the WIGGLE-related changes you can't actually see, a system made up of specialized brain cells called mirror neurons is fully developed within roughly the first 12 months. These unique neurons allow babies' brains to practice the motor movements they see others around them making even before they can physically master the motor milestones for themselves.

12 months

"Up and at 'em!" This is the age defined by the ability to pull to a stand and walk holding on to furniture, both of which afford children entering toddlerhood an even better view of, not to mention access to, the world around them. Fine motor skills start to appear as well, with 12-month-olds now able to pick things up by using their thumb and index finger (known as the "pincer grasp"). This milestone further enhances their ability to explore and, of course, put things in their mouths—a regular occurrence that, for children this age, continues to be essentially synonymous with exploring. Cognitively, they can now grasp that when you hide an object, it still exists.

15 months

In addition to walking more independently—typically taking a few steps on their own—and fine-tuning the use of their hands (most notably to finger-feed themselves), 15-month-olds continue to demonstrate that physical development goes hand in hand with cognitive development. This can be seen in the cognitive milestones characteristic of this age: trying to use objects like a phone, cup or book in the "right" way, and figuring out how to stack blocks and other small objects.

18 months

Add climbing, scribbling, drinking from a cup (albeit with the occasional spill), and attempting to use a spoon to the list of what 18-month-olds are typically able to do, in addition to perfecting their ability to walk all by themselves without needing to hold on to anything or anyone. Along with the mastery of so many new motor milestones comes their enhanced cognitive ability to not just interact with but to actually play with toys, and to learn from and copy adult activities such as sweeping with a broom.

Two years

By age two, children are typically off and running (literally), and also add kicking balls and walking up stairs to their list of abilities. With new and improved ways to get around and physically interact with the world, they test out switches, knobs and buttons on toys, play with more than one at a time, and can more intentionally hold things in one hand so they can use the other to explore it—for example, holding a container in one hand while removing the lid with the other.

30 months

Two-and-a-half-year-olds are typically able to use their hands to twist things (such as doorknobs and lids), jump with both feet off the ground, and turn the pages of a book one at a time. Cognitive milestones continue to be defined by improved movement capabilities as children at this age demonstrate their ability to pretend through the hands-on use of toys and objects; their budding problem-solving abilities by using a step stool to reach something; and their ability to follow two-step instructions by getting up and going through the motions of doing them (for example, putting a toy down and closing a door as instructed).

Three years

In a continued blending of motor and cognitive milestones, three-year-olds can do all sorts of new things: draw circles (when shown how), string items together, put some types of clothes on for themselves, use a fork, and even know, once warned, not to explore hot objects by touching them (an understanding that, of course, should not be relied upon without putting additional safety measures in place). "Doing the hustle" accurately describes the motor abilities of three-year-olds: they busily and physically explore books, puzzles and blocks; learn to work toys with buttons, levers and moving parts; climb well, run easily, and get up and down stairs in a more coordinated way by placing only one foot on each step.

Four and five years

Now generally able to hop, skip, kick, spin, throw, catch, and move forward, backward, and up and down with steadily improving agility, pre-kindergarteners are ready for all sorts of action, both physically and cognitively speaking. In terms of officially designated milestones, their abilities include catching large balls, serving themselves food and pouring water with supervision, drawing, unbuttoning at least some types of buttons, and holding crayons or pencils between their fingers and thumbs rather than in a fist.

STAGE	WIGGLE MILESTONES
Newborn	involuntary reflexes and little intentional control, mirror neurons, watching and learning
2–4 months	holds head up, controls more movements, coordinates hand-eye movement
4–6 months	starting to roll and to sit means the start of increased access
9–12 months	"up and at 'em": from sitting to standing to walking, pincer grasp
1–2 years	shaking, banging, throwing, walking, improved fine motor skills and use of fingers
3 years	busily and physically exploring toys; more coordinated running, climbing
4–5 years	ready to explore: hop, skip, kick, spin, throw, catch, and move forward, backward, up and down with improved agility

CLASSROOM QI-NNECTIONS
Embracing a hands-on approach to WIGGLE

The best way to encourage WIGGLE Skills development in your classroom is to embrace this easy-to-remember concept: *the more hands-on it is, the better*. Looking and listening have long been encouraged in the early years, but so too should touching, poking, feeling, moving, taking apart and, when appropriate, smelling and tasting. It's these sorts of hands-on, mind-engaged type of activities that work best.

ENHANCING ACTIVE
ENGAGEMENT WITH WIGGLE

Shortly after I had been brought in to introduce and discuss QI Skills in the early childhood classroom at an annual professional development day, the owner of the center called me up to tell me just how much she and her teachers appreciated what I had shared with them. Of course, I was thrown a bit when she proceeded to tell me that one of her best, most long-standing teachers had come into her office the following day, proclaiming "I am a terrible teacher!"

This was the last thing I wanted to hear, given that my goal was and is to empower teachers. I quickly started to apologize, saying something to the effect of, "Oh no! That was *not* my intent," when the owner shared the rest of the story. The teacher had come to admit to the owner that she hadn't been letting the children in her classroom WIGGLE. It turns out that this fabulous preschool teacher, after reflecting on what I'd shared about active young children and WIGGLE, realized that her efforts to keep her classroom orderly, neat and quiet came with unintended consequences.

Upon learning about WIGGLE, she actively committed to creating more WIGGLE room in her classroom and throughout each day. The result? Sure, her classroom was a little messier and, at times, a bit louder. But the increase in decibels could mostly be accounted for by the increased laughter of her far more actively engaged students. The teacher also found she was much less stressed now that she was no longer faced with the unrealistic challenge of trying to keep everyone sitting perfectly still.

As with most of the QI Skills, developing children's WIGGLE Skills is less about active facilitation than simply providing them the necessary space, time, and encouragement to physically interact with the world around them. As we've discussed, when left to their own devices even newborn babies are naturally wired to practice their WIGGLE Skills as they first squirm, but then quickly develop the ability to reach for, grab, touch, crawl, walk and run towards things they want to explore. In fact, I suggest to you that adults and children alike learn best (not to mention strengthen our QI Skills) through active, hands-on learning. Sure, letting children WIGGLE more will likely require a bit more thought, safety-proofing, time and supervision. But in the long run, it's well worth it. Rather than simply working to get their WIGGLES out, your role as an early educator can and should be to help children put their WIGGLES to work. Here are some easy ways for you to help them get going:

Activities
* **Recognize WIGGLE when you see it**. Understanding that physical and cognitive learning go hand in hand—and what that looks like—is the first step. Once you know what to look for, you will be better able to appreciate children's early attempts to WIGGLE (i.e., reach, touch, take apart, play with, poke or grab) for what they are. Be sure to take notice of the WIGGLE involved when an infant discovers their hands or reaches for a toy hanging from their activity gym for the first time. Continue to recognize the value of WIGGLE as children become more mobile, increasingly get into things and, as a result, are more likely to keep you on your toes throughout the day.

- **Swaddle with care.** Swaddling, by definition, generally involves wrapping babies in a blanket. Although there are different permutations, this often includes wrapping arms, legs and all, and doing so fairly snugly so that babies' natural reflexes won't cause them to wriggle free. Swaddling is a popular strategy for calming babies and helping them sleep, and understandably so given its sleep-inducing results. However, be aware that swaddling also stands to restrict WIGGLE. To avoid inadvertently suppressing WIGGLE, avoid swaddling babies when they're awake and active. Instead of relying solely on swaddling for daytime calming, turn to other effective methods for soothing, such as singing or rocking, and reserve swaddling primarily for sleep, and only during the first three to four months.

WIGGLE VS. SWADDLE

According to the American Academy of Pediatrics, it's okay to swaddle babies so long as you make sure they're not swaddled too tightly; always place them on their backs when swaddled; never use a weighted blanket; and commit to stop swaddling when they look like they're trying to roll over (usually around three to four months).[80]

Of course, you'll also want to take into account any local and state licensing requirements, given the sleep safety concerns that swaddling raises. The Office of Child Care at the Administration for Children and Families states that "swaddling is not recommended and shall require a note from the child's physician if continued past the age of three months."[81]

- **Create plenty of WIGGLE rooms.** The public perception of well-run classrooms often does not include nearly enough time or space to WIGGLE. Childproofing is essential for creating WIGGLE room while also ensuring young children stay safe. When classrooms, playgrounds and other play spaces are properly childproofed, it gives you the peace of mind needed to allow children to move around and explore much more freely and regularly. Remember also to make sure that the floors are clean and have play mats conducive for WIGGLE-ing.

- **Allow for active reading.** For children who find it hard to sit still—i.e., the majority of toddlers and preschoolers—there are many things you can do to more actively engage them in reading. These include letting them point to illustrations, hold the book, turn pages, and draw related pictures. Another fun option involves reading "active" books (some examples of which can be found in QI References and Resources at the back of this book) and allowing children to get up and act them out as you read, miming the actions in books like *The Itsy, Bitsy Spider; Jump, Frog, Jump!*; and *Wheels on the Bus.* For other children (my own three included), simply offering them the chance to quietly build puzzles, color pictures, create beaded crafts, or any of a whole host of other age-appropriate manipulative options may be more than enough to enhance their engagement with the story (not to mention their attention span), while also providing them with the opportunity to fidget, move and WIGGLE.

EMBODIED READING

The motto for cognitive psychologist Art Glenberg's Embodied Cognition Lab at Arizona State University is "I act, therefore I am." Among the WIGGLE-related areas of research in which his lab is actively engaged, Glenberg's "Moved by Reading" intervention has demonstrated notable gains in learning—both in emerging readers' memory and their comprehension—as a result of simply encouraging children to physically manipulate toys to simulate the content of what they're reading.[82] [83]

- **Beware of withholding WIGGLE.** In light of all we know about the benefits of WIGGLE, we should all think twice before deciding to withhold the opportunity for children to get up and move. Think about the preschooler who's not allowed to play outside because they won't sit still, follow directions and focus in the classroom. Unfortunately, it's not uncommon for fidgety, WIGGLE-y children to be punished by restricting their activity, when the reality is that they're the ones whose focus and attention could likely benefit most from being able to move around freely.

- **Run free.** From the time toddlers learn how to pick up speed, it's easy as an early educator to fall into the trap of routinely telling them, "Don't run!" This cautionary command was once reserved for occasions where safety was of paramount concern, like near a street or in a crowded public place. In cases where it doesn't serve a clear purpose, however, the frequent use of this command runs counter to what we hope to cultivate in children when it comes to WIGGLE-ing their way to success. As a mom, pediatrician, and early education professional, I've certainly seen my fair share of skinned knees and bitten lips that result from running-related trips and falls. But I'll be the first to confirm that in a great many instances, the benefits of letting children run far outweigh the potential risks (which, most of the time, can be made better with some TLC and a Band-Aid). By creating environments in which children can literally and figuratively run free whenever possible, you can help them learn from a very young age how their bodies can move and be used to explore the world.

WHAT WIGGLE ISN'T

Whenever I advocate for letting children WIGGLE, I always imagine there's a teacher or two inevitably thinking to themselves that I must not understand what it takes to keep an early childhood classroom running smoothly. Allow me to assure you that I do. Letting a child WIGGLE does not mean letting them bounce off the walls—a circumstance that I fully acknowledge is in no way conducive to learning for either the out-of-control child or the rest of the students who are unable to concentrate as a result of the frenzied environment. What allowing young children to WIGGLE *does* mean, however, is loosening the reins enough to allow them to truly learn and explore. That applies to the early childhood equivalent of "seat time" and, for example, significantly limiting how long children are expected to sit "crisscross applesauce" in a designated spot without moving, touching, poking or otherwise interacting with the subject at hand.

- **Explore the great outdoors.** Stepping outside your classroom provides children with limitless opportunities for simultaneously moving, learning and exploring the natural world, whether through playing, running, taking nature walks or outdoor field trips, or simply collecting sticks, pine cones or leaves.

- **Beware of the strapped-in temptation.** Give serious thought to how much time infants and toddlers in your care are spending in strollers, bouncy seats, highchairs, car seats, or any other types of contraptions that limit their movement. These straps come with a price, limiting children's first and foundational abilities to move and explore. Yes, there will be times when safety, time or circumstances won't allow it, but remember that the opportunity to take lots of baby steps inevitably leads to bigger and better things.

- **Embrace the WIGGLE.** If your image of a "perfect" preschool classroom is one defined by calm, quiet and orderly behavior, I hope you'll look at things a bit differently after adding some WIGGLE to this picture. Although there's a time for quiet and for sitting still, it's equally important that there be time for running, jumping and exploring (accompanied by a potential increase in mess and noise). A well-thought-out early childhood classroom should not just tolerate, but be set up to provide children ample opportunities to do both.

- **Put WIGGLES to work.** Playing active games such as "Duck, Duck, Goose," "Simon Says," and tag naturally encourages preschoolers to be physically active while learning, demonstrating how they can exercise a whole host of QI Skills, including ME, WE, and WOBBLE (more on the latter in the next chapter). Even babies and toddlers can actively participate in WIGGLE activities as simple as singing songs like pat-a-cake, "Head, Shoulders, Knees and Toes," or "Itsy Bitsy Spider"—all of which allow the words to be brought to life and better understood by physically acting them out.

QI TAKEAWAYS: WIGGLE

- WIGGLE Skills represent the concepts of hands-on and embodied learning, and the recognition that physical and intellectual restlessness go hand in hand.

- WIGGLE Skills show how dynamic motion is integral to learning about the world and actively engaging with it.

- WIGGLE Skills involve being physically active not only to improve physical fitness, but also to enhance creative thought and overall readiness to learn.

- Achieving WIGGLE success is not simply a matter of helping children work their WIGGLEs out, but of helping them learn how best to put their WIGGLEs to work.

- Insisting young children sit perfectly still and control their physical impulses places competing demands on the same part of the brain (the prefrontal cortex) responsible for actively paying attention, making it that much harder to do either well.

- When you think of WIGGLE Skills, think of the phrase "hands-on, minds on."[84]

QI REFLECTIONS: WIGGLE

- Are you more inclined to think of WIGGLE-ing as a skill, or a classroom challenge? What do you picture when you think about a classroom where WIGGLE-ing is allowed? How does it look, sound, and feel different from the way you currently run your classroom?

- What would you need to do or change to make your classroom and/or curriculum more conducive to WIGGLE-ing?

- Think about a child in your class who might be "high energy." Consider and list ways you could help them put their WIGGLEs to work, allowing them to be more actively and successfully engaged in your typical daily routines and activities.

- Think of a time in your life when you engaged in hands-on learning. When and where did it take place? How did it feel? How was it different from other educational experiences that weren't hands-on? Did you find it to be helpful? More fun and interesting?

WOBBLE
Failing to Succeed—Raising
Children Who are Fit to Fail

"There is no innovation and
creativity without failure."

BRENÉ BROWN

I N 1971, the Playskool division of the Hasbro toy company introduced Weebles®. Over the decades, these immensely popular egg-shaped, bottom-heavy toys have come in an impressively wide variety of styles, but all share one defining feature: they always return to their upright position after they're pushed, tipped or tossed. More than 50 years and millions of Weebles later, this classic toy has been recognized by *Time* Magazine as one of its All-TIME 100 Greatest Toys,[85] while its ever-so-catchy slogan, "Weebles wobble, but they don't fall down," has remained firmly embedded in the minds of generations of children and parents.[86] That Weebles repeatedly teeter and falter but bounce back upright is the very quality that forms the foundation for this chapter's QI Skill: WOBBLE.

In a figurative sense, being able to WOBBLE yet ultimately remain standing represents a crucial ability today: the ability to embrace the risk of making mistakes, learn from them, and continuously strive to accomplish new feats that are beyond one's current capacities. In today's increasingly complex and rapidly changing world, the need to learn and be encouraged to try out all sorts of new and daring ideas, falter, fail, and bounce back up wiser and more resilient than before is critical.

Like the weight built into every Weeble to anchor it, the key to supporting children's WOBBLE Skills lies in providing them with a firm but flexible foundation that supports them as they learn to embrace, rebound and learn from failures, and explore, adapt, discover and innovate. As you might imagine, embracing WOBBLE also facilitates the development of other foundational QI Skills, especially the WHAT IF Skills so crucial to cultivating creativity and encouraging innovation that I'll be introducing in the next chapter.

> ● **WOBBLE Skills** are the adaptability skills necessary to support, build, and foster intelligent risk-taking, perseverance, resilience, adaptability, agility, and the ability to face, overcome, and learn from failure.

What's in a WOBBLE?

Of all the future-ready skills that the QI Skills framework was created to describe and define, WOBBLE is the one that seems to resonate most strongly with business leaders as the skill they're most likely to look for in a new hire. That shouldn't come as much of a surprise when you consider which skills are most likely to be important during times of rapid change.

In an AI-powered world where many of the old, familiar, tried-and-true rules and ways of doing things no longer apply, and where you're more likely than ever to be faced with lots of new challenges and questions that don't have easy answers, what becomes really important is one's willingness and ability to fail, adapt, and try again. I'm fairly convinced, however, that this is not the only reason this QI Skill has become so highly valued: I suspect it also has a lot to do with the fact that WOBBLE (like the word "QI") gives a single, proper name to an otherwise long, haphazard list of clearly recognized and highly desirable skills, attributes, and abilities that are all unquestionably valuable. WOBBLE Skills include:

- Intelligent risk-taking
- Adaptability
- Agility
- Willingness to try new things
- Perseverance
- Resilience
- Grit
- Overcoming obstacles
- Learning from failure

In addition to serving as a unifying term for an assortment of highly coveted skills, the concept of WOBBLE also aims to remove the stigma of failure. Framing these skills in this way offers everyone from early childhood educators to business executives a fresh way to look at the inevitable trials children and adults face as learning opportunities.

The rise of failure

Failure has long gotten a bad rap. In school, business, science, politics and sports, not to mention in our personal lives, tremendous value has been placed on "getting it right." Failure, in contrast, has typically been regarded as something to be embarrassed about and avoided at all costs.

"Failure is not an option"—a phrase popularized by the 1995 movie *Apollo 13*—has become a concerningly pervasive sentiment. Children and adults alike who become adept at dodging failure are more likely to be recognized, praised and rewarded. It's no wonder so many children are growing up hesitant to take chances and unwilling to test new approaches and take on new challenges or set stretch goals. To advance in a world where any amount of WOBBLE is perceived as weakness, it's only natural to want to appear upright and steady, sticking to and showcasing what we already know how to do.

But, as with the world around us, things are changing when it comes to embracing failure, and they're changing fast. In large part, this is because failure is increasingly becoming recognized as essential for innovation. In fact, it's frequently noted that if you can't afford to fail, you can't afford to innovate—which is an especially big obstacle in a world where innovative thinking is in such high demand. In this recognition that failure is going to be an inherent part of addressing the complex, yet-to-be-solved problems of today and tomorrow, an intriguing shift in thinking has started to appear across the worlds of business, entrepreneurship, leadership and innovation: instead of instinctively avoiding failure, leaders, managers, investors and organizations (along with forward-thinking educators) have made it a point to lean into and place increasingly high value on the ability to embrace and learn from failure, and lean on those best able to do so.

....

"Many people think you get
stability by minimizing all risk. But
ironically, in a changing world, that's
one of the riskiest things you can do."

REID HOFFMAN

The Start-up of You

....

Many employers now routinely question job applicants about their past failures. But instead of just considering those as black marks on a potential employee's record, they're seeking to determine if that individual possesses coveted WOBBLE Skills, like grit and perseverance, which are so critical to take on challenges in today's world of work.

When you start looking around, you see the signs of this shift are everywhere. Google, for example, formalized the thoughtful rewarding of failure as one of its key "Principles of Innovation"[87] over a decade ago: encouraging employees to try lots of things "often and early" without striving for perfection, advocating for the ability to "fail well," and generally creating a workplace environment and culture where failure is treated as a badge of honor.

Higher education has followed suit. Students applying to college are no longer asked to simply list their awards, grades, scores and accomplishments: rather, they are likely to find themselves faced with questions like, "Recount an incident or time when you experienced failure. How did it affect you, and what lessons did you learn?" Upon entering college, students today may well be encouraged to write a "failure resume," laying out past setbacks and how they responded to them; be offered formal programs focused on "Failing Well"[88] or take a course like "Failure 101," an actual engineering lab course that required students to take risks and experiment with an understanding that the more they failed, the better their chances of receiving an A in the course.[89] Despite all it has had working against it, failure has finally managed to acquire a potentially positive connotation, with the ability to overcome and learn from it now established as a highly sought-after skill.

WOBBLE in action

In spite of this shift toward embracing failure, many early educators still struggle with allowing any WOBBLE in their classrooms, much less making it a regular facet of their curricula. Parents, and our safety- and success-driven culture as a whole, also tend to be understandably reluctant to let WOBBLE happen, especially when children are young. After all, what seems like a good idea in theory is admittedly difficult to watch, much less embrace, when it involves a toddler teetering, tipping over, and all but inevitably tumbling. Rather than recognizing WOBBLE as a valuable skill-in-the-making and nurturing children's natural willingness to test, explore, fall down, get up and try again, it's all too easy to succumb to a culture committed to both getting it right, and caught up in the need to protect children from failure and upset at all costs, no matter how minor.

Let me take a moment to make very clear that I'm the last person to discount the importance of injury prevention and "cushioning the blows" of early childhood. Things like bike helmets, car seats, and always laying babies to sleep on their backs in safe sleep spaces are strongly recommended for good reason, and are all very worthwhile safety measures. There's no question that we must continue to implement these sorts of measures to protect children from serious, crash-and-burn type failures, as those types of "failure" are *not* what we're talking about when we talk about WOBBLE.

I would suggest, however, that we do need to seek more balance in our approach to letting children experience the kind of failure from which they stand to not just recover, but learn. In her book *The Blessing of a Skinned Knee*, psychologist Wendy Mogul warns against the kind of overprotectiveness that involves attempting to prevent children from experiencing even the slightest stumble, scrape or upset.[90] Yes, it is literally in your job description as an early educator (not to mention spelled out in your childcare licensing requirements) to provide children with a safe environment. But as early educators committed to equipping children with the tools and strategies they'll need to succeed in school, work and life, you also need to afford them the opportunity to, as per the unofficial motto of Silicon Valley, "fail early, fail often and ultimately fail forward."

Spaghetti and marshmallows: A test of WOBBLE

If you accept the concept of "failing well"—that is, embracing the idea that making mistakes and coming up short are all part of learning and growing—you must also be able to assess your own willingness to take risks and fail. One of my favorite ways of testing that willingness is through a popular activity called "the Marshmallow Challenge." As distinct from the Mischel experiment we discussed in the ME chapter, this is routinely referred to as the "Spaghetti Marshmallow Challenge." It's an activity I've enjoyed both participating in and facilitating for participants of all ages and professions over the years.

Here's how it works. Participants are divided into teams of four or five. Set on a table in front of each team is one large marshmallow, 20 uncooked spaghetti noodles, a yard of string, a yard of tape, and a pair of scissors. Using only these supplies, each team has 18 minutes to build a free-standing tower. The goal is to build the tallest tower that can support the full weight of the marshmallow, placed on top, without toppling.

Who do you think would be especially good at this challenging task? What attributes might you look for? The ages, educational background and professional experiences of the team members, perhaps? Tom Wujec, a globally recognized thought leader on creativity, design, and strategy, has conducted many such Spaghetti Marshmallow Challenge competitions, and what he found in assessing the results was both instructive and probably a bit different than what you might guess. It was, in fact, teams of recent *kindergarten* graduates on average who performed particularly well at this tower-building task. By comparison, recent business and law school graduates were the least impressive. The only two types of teams Wujec found outperformed the kindergarteners were (1) engineers and architects (thank goodness!), and (2) CEOs—but only when they had administrative assistants on their team.[91]

The reason I am so fond of introducing this activity to early educators is not only because it spotlights children's abilities, but also because it naturally leads just about everyone to wonder why it is that young children are better able to handle this complex assignment than so many highly educated and experienced adults. You might be asking yourself the same question: What's going on?

The answer is, lots of things. Certainly, WE Skills come into play in a challenge where teamwork, communication and quick collaboration are so obviously central to success. One might even speculate that perhaps CEO-only teams don't fare as well because leaders tend to be better at giving directions than playing well with others; as Wujec speculated in his TED Talk, kindergarteners don't spend time trying to be "CEO of Spaghetti Inc."[92] But there are far more than just WE Skills at work here.

While all of the QI Skills actually come into play in the Spaghetti Marshmallow Challenge, for the purposes of this chapter it's worth noting that the key WOBBLE abilities the young children displayed can be formally described as rapid iteration and prototyping—terms that come straight from a human-centered approach called design thinking. Of course, this innovation-culture jargon means nothing to children (or most early educators, for that matter). But what does matter is that this challenge helps us to more clearly see that young children—better than all but a select few categories of adults—possess an innate and eager willingness to try new things, to fail, to adapt, and to try again. If this has you thinking back to WILL Skills, it should. WILL Skills are a driver both for building the tower as well as the aspect of WOBBLE that involves being okay enough with failing to try again.

Consider that kindergarteners were found to make, on average, five separate attempts to build their marshmallow towers during their allotted 18 minutes, each serving to inform their next steps and ultimately winning strategy. Contrast their efforts with newly minted MBAs who, on average, made only one attempt. This is not all that surprising, given that traditional business school training often emphasizes the ability to search for, find, and implement the one single right answer. When faced with an unknown and challenging task, both recent business and law school graduates (and a whole lot of other highly educated adults) tend to spend a majority of their allotted time debating and drawing on pre-existing assumptions in an attempt to get it right on the first try, only to try once—and fail—to execute their "perfect" solution just before time runs out.

Think about how many years, not to mention how much time, money and effort, goes into educating the WOBBLE that comes so naturally to young children out of these "highly trained" professionals, and you'll understand why we need to recognize, protect and cultivate these skills. To that end, let's now take a look at how *not* to train the WOBBLE out of them!

Learning to fail forward

As the Spaghetti Marshmallow Challenge reveals, young children are naturally quite adept at trying new things, failing, learning from their mistakes, and adapting. They just need your support to safely learn how to fail forward. These factors are key to WOBBLE Skill development.

This means not making children feel inadequate or slow because they haven't yet mastered a particular task or ability. Instead, recognize their efforts when they fall short of a goal. Notice when they're overly fearful about taking a harmless tumble, and encourage them to take the leap (figuratively and literally). I understand this is a big shift and a tall order in a world where focus has typically been solely placed (and often misplaced, in my opinion) on children's ability to get something right. But it's worth the effort required to take a different course to cultivate lifelong WOBBLE Skills.

WOBBLE TOWARD A GROWTH MINDSET

Placing a disproportionate amount of focus on what children achieve quickly or on the first try encourages them to limit their efforts to only those tasks they know they can easily accomplish. This will make them more likely to shy away from new or challenging activities, and develop what Stanford psychologist and best-selling author Carol Dweck defines as a fixed mindset. Instead, you should encourage children to welcome new challenges irrespective of whether they can meet them successfully on the first try, and take pride in the effort they put forth to persevere. By embracing some degree of failure as integral to learning, WOBBLE Skills can lead to what Dweck describes as a growth mindset.

DEVELOPMENTAL MILESTONES
WOBBLE behind the scenes

As a fundamentally important QI Skill, WOBBLE turns out to be a bit of an anomaly when it comes to recognizable developmental milestones. That's because, unlike the other QI Skills, WOBBLE doesn't neatly align with the standard way of charting a child's developmental course.

This is because milestones, technically speaking, are measures of success. When a child reaches a milestone, it means they've achieved it, and you (or their parents) can make note of the date and check it off as having been successfully accomplished. But WOBBLE-ing, by definition, consists of all of the behind-the-scenes failed attempts and adaptations that eventually lead to achieving those milestones. In other words, working on one's WOBBLE involves *not* succeeding. From a developmental standpoint, another way to think about it is that WOBBLE Skills represent the process rather than the end result.

Just because there aren't formally defined developmental milestones for each stage of WOBBLE doesn't mean, however, that young children aren't using WOBBLE Skills almost from the time they're born. When given the chance, they literally spend all day, every day, engaging in trial-and-error—trying, failing, adapting, failing and trying again. This is what ultimately leads them to master all the classic childhood developmental milestones, from holding their heads up and rolling over to pushing themselves up, crawling, walking, and talking.

It's also what should motivate you to make sure that children are provided ample opportunity to WOBBLE. Given the pressures to document young children's successes, now more than ever early educators run the risk of overlooking children's WOBBLE, as well as overprotecting, overcompensating, and unnecessarily shielding them from failure. Below are a few examples of WOBBLE Skills in action.

> "Do not judge me by my successes,
> judge me by how many times
> I fell down and got back up again"
>
> **NELSON MANDELA**

What WOBBLE-ing looks like

Self-feeding with a spoon. Children don't typically master the much-anticipated milestone of spoon-feeding themselves with any real degree of accuracy until somewhere around two years of age, but that doesn't mean they don't spend a whole lot of time (when given the chance) trying. Expect a lot of near-misses and at least as many spills and messes. Remember to celebrate (and even commemorate with a photograph or two) their blossoming WOBBLE Skills and the many unsuccessful attempts that, in the short run, may leave food everywhere except the spoon's intended target.

Toddling. Pretty much by definition, toddling implies that a child is learning but has not yet mastered the coveted skill of walking—a process that clearly involves a significant degree of WOBBLE-ing. Early attempts at mastery are invariably marked by trips and tumbles. By the end of the first year, some children still spend more time on the ground than on their feet. Others—the early walkers—refuse to settle for simply pulling themselves to a standing position and cruising by holding onto furniture. Instead, they go straight from making it onto their feet to attempting to walk without relying on any cautionary steps, handholding, or other supports. These hardcore WOBBLE-ers insist on trying to walk, taking more than their fair share of tumbles, but are more than willing to keep trying if only we clear a safe path and let them.

Self-dressing. The "failures" involved in self-dressing are many (and often comically hard to miss). This includes mismatched socks, shoes on the wrong feet, odd pairings of shirts and pants, and struggles with buttons and snaps.

Reciting the alphabet. This is one of my favorite go-to examples for reminding early educators to stop and simply recognize and appreciate overlooked WOBBLE Skills in action. After all, no one expects young children to master the alphabet suddenly without any practice or trial-and-error. Rather, we start singing the alphabet to very young babies, and enthusiastically encourage their attempts to imitate us. These attempts invariably start as little more than mouth movements and coos, progressing over time to vaguely musical mumbles and slurred sounds that faintly resemble the names of the letters. Technically speaking, these early attempts could be considered failures. It can take years of such "failed efforts"—predictably struggling with the enunciation of certain sequences of letters (think *l, m, n, o*), putting them in the wrong order, saying them incorrectly, and repeating some while leaving out others—before the persistence of WOBBLE ultimately leads children successfully from *a* all the way to *z*.

CLASSROOM QI-NNECTIONS
Setting WOBBLE Skills in motion

You can help young children develop WOBBLE by taking a number of actions while refraining from others. As with WIGGLE Skills and creating a conducive *physical* environment, the key with WOBBLE is to create a *learning* environment where children not only feel encouraged to explore, test things out, and try lots of new behaviors, but to do so safely and without the fear of, unnecessary risks associated with, or serious repercussions from making mistakes. The following are a sampling of activities—some admittedly a bit messier, more time-consuming, or less orderly than others—that can help you achieve this goal.

Activities

• **WOBBLE-proof your classroom.** Otherwise known as safety-proofing, WOBBLE-proofing is as much for you as for children when it comes to allowing both WIGGLE and WOBBLE to happen. While safety-proofing children's surroundings helps protect them from serious injury, it comes with the added benefit of giving you the peace of mind necessary to be able to comfortably step back and let young children explore... and WOBBLE! Remember that a certain low level of risk is necessary to support WOBBLE and healthy development in general. This doesn't include the kind of unnecessary risks that can and should be prevented with locked cabinets, finger-safe doors, and firmly affixing furniture to the wall to keep it from tipping. But it does allow for the kind of messes, spills, bumps and bruises associated with all of the carrying, touching, taking apart and building children are able to do when provided a safe space in which to actively experiment and explore.

FEAR NOT THE "F-WORDS"

Helping children make the most of their WOBBLES involves adjusting one's perspective on failure. It also requires resisting the instinct to protect them from ever experiencing a whole host of additional "f-words" like "fall," "falter," "fumble," and "flail" in the name of keeping them safe from all physical or emotional "harm."

- **Allow children to fail early and often**. It's the *early and often* part of this prescription that can admittedly be a bit difficult to embrace. A classic example is learning to walk: you may worry that you'll be seen as negligent if you sit back and watch as a toddler takes a few tumbles while they're in your care. Or, you might feel like you should immediately help an infant settle back down in the crib the first time they pull to a stand during naptime but haven't yet figured out how to lower themselves back down to sleep. These kinds of concerns are perfectly understandable. But when you make a commitment to tolerating an early-and-often recoverable failure regimen, it means you need to give children of all ages the opportunity to try and figure things out for themselves. Strengthening children's WOBBLE abilities involves accepting that minor falls and bumps are bound to happen without resulting in any real harm, and committing to helping them learn to brush themselves off and rebound from manageable failures.

DON'T TAKE IT TOO HARD

Although my firstborn was a generally cautious toddler, she still had her fair share of tumbles when she was first learning to walk. On occasion, these tumbles would result in what my husband and I came to call "head bonks"—those distressing but generally harmless knocks to the head (i.e., the kind that don't involve falls from high places, sharp corners, loss of consciousness, or any other more potentially serious injuries). Even with all our combined years

> of medical training, it admittedly still took some effort to not overreact and try to prevent her from ever falling or keep from running to her immediate rescue whenever she faltered. To encourage her WOBBLE-ing, we instead made a game of teaching our daughter to brush off these head bumps (not to mention develop an early sense of humor) by saying "cuckoo, cuckoo."

- **Find the balance between risky and risk**. The former means allowing young children to play unsupervised near a busy street; the latter means allowing preschoolers to climb on age-appropriate playground equipment knowing that they might fall. Thinking in terms of balance can help you keep children in the WOBBLE zone—right-sizing the risk involved in allowing them to try, learn from, and even fail at new and ever-more-challenging, but also worthwhile and rewarding experiences.

- **Celebrate mistakes and failures**. As early educators focused on helping children thrive, it's understandable that we often focus our greatest enthusiasm on successes and achievements like first words, first steps, and learning to read and write. However, it's equally important to show similar excitement over creative or noble-but-unsuccessful early attempts, failures, and adaptations in everyday activities. This could involve anything from stacking building blocks that fall over, to coloring (even if outside the lines), to attempting to say new words.

  Clap your hands, voice encouragement, and remember to celebrate when you see children persist in the face of "failure." When my nephew was in kindergarten, for example, his enlightened teacher praised students' willingness to WOBBLE by having the class join her in cheering "hip, hip, hooray, we have a risk-taker in class today!" This sort of demonstrated support for efforts involving trying new things and risk with a purpose can go a long way toward encouraging young children's willingness to WOBBLE. After all, the goal is to have children grow up believing that making mistakes is not the opposite of success. Rather, learning from one's mistakes is an invaluable part of the process that ultimately paves the way to success!

- **Prioritize problem-solving.** One of the first and most impactful steps we can take to help children engage in problem-solving is to let them actually tackle some kid-size problems. For example, let them work through, however haphazardly, building, making, or constructing something as they see fit. Allow them to navigate social interactions with their classmates, such as sharing and taking turns, understanding that they won't always succeed. Instead of letting children interpret these problematic occurrences as upsetting or frustrating failures, turn them into opportunities for students to learn how to discuss what happened, why it happened, how it made those involved feel, and what could be done differently going forward to change the outcome to a more successful one. This plays directly into a key concept of WOBBLE: the valuable skill here is not just experiencing failure, but developing the ability to learn from it.

- **Partner with parents.** Creating an early childhood classroom environment in which young children are not just able but actively encouraged to try new things, fail, and learn by making lots of "great mistakes" requires not only time, encouragement, and some strategic safety-proofing, but also buy-in from parents. By sharing with parents how and why you encourage all of the making, sharing, and learning from mistakes that go into WOBBLE, you can help ensure that they see the value as well. This can also help prevent the perception that in allowing their children to make mistakes or fail without intervening, you are somehow not doing your job.

- **Make time for WOBBLE.** Plain and simple, it takes time to WOBBLE. This means that WOBBLE development can often be enhanced by simply removing unnecessarily rigid time constraints and allowing young children the extra time needed to assess, explore, and attempt new strategies for completing tasks, tackling challenges, or mastering new skills.

QI TAKEAWAYS: WOBBLE

- WOBBLE-ing involves being willing to take risks, try new things, and take on challenging tasks, with the understanding that success isn't always dependent on how fast or even *if* you accomplish what you set out to do, but rather on how much you learn in the process.

- WOBBLE Skills are less about the end result and more about mastering the ability to wrestle with, be challenged by, spend time on, and learn from challenging tasks.

- Supporting WOBBLE is about encouraging intelligent risk-taking. It's *not* about stepping back and allowing children to take unnecessary or dangerous risks or experience massive failure.

- Failing, in and of itself, is not a valuable skill. What is of significant value is the learning, understanding, and adapting that comes from it. In other words, WOBBLE is not simply about making mistakes, but learning from them.

- WOBBLE Skills lack definable developmental milestones for the simple reason that milestones, by definition, represent successes. WOBBLE Skills, by contrast, represent all of the risk-taking, perseverance, mistakes, failed attempts, and overcoming of obstacles that go into ultimately mastering the milestone moments.

- Remember that a certain low level of risk is necessary to cultivate WOBBLE Skills.

QI REFLECTIONS: WOBBLE

- Can you think of any ways in which you could, either now or in the future, make taking chances and making mistakes not just allowable, but encouraged and celebrated in your classroom?

- Think about a time when you made a mistake, or when something didn't go as planned in your classroom. How did you react? In what ways did you use (or could you have used) this circumstance to model WOBBLE Skills for your students? What might you say? How might you describe what happened and your approach to learning from failure?

- In what ways do the requirements of your job, your curriculum, and your daily routines serve to support and encourage you to WOBBLE? Which of these elements do you see as potential obstacles or constraints when it comes to allowing WOBBLE to happen?

- Think about how you approach making mistakes and failure. Consider one or two specific examples from your life, and then make a list of words that describe how each made you feel. Now think about what you do with these feelings: do they tend to motivate you, or do they make you more likely to avoid those challenges or circumstances where success isn't guaranteed?

WHAT IF
Imagining a World
of Possibilities

. . . .

"Creativity is intelligence having fun."

ALBERT EINSTEIN

IN THIS, the final of the QI Skill Chapters, you are going to be introduced to a set of skills that I like to think of as the culmination of the QI Skills: WHAT IF Skills. You'll soon see all the ways WHAT IF Skills are integral and can be cultivated throughout early childhood, and I'll share examples of how you can apply WHAT IF in your classroom.

In today's world, where we live so much of our lives online, you don't have to look much further than how many likes, shares or views a social media post garners to get a taste of what captures people's attention at any given moment. Now, consider TED—the global organization that hosts and then posts online ideas worth spreading in the form of what now totals nearly 50,000 short videos covering an impressively wide range of topics, collected from over 10,000 events around the world. TED's most-watched video of all time is one that has drawn more than 77 million viewers, and it's striking, not to mention WHAT IF–relevant, that the star of this particular "viral" video isn't a cat playing with yarn, a celebrity, or some random person performing a cringe-worthy stunt gone awry. Rather, it's the late British international education adviser and author Sir Kenneth Robinson, whose talk happens to be squarely focused on a key component of WHAT IF—namely, the question, "Do schools kill creativity?"[93] Even before setting aside 20 minutes to actually watch it for yourself (which is worth doing), the talk's massive global reach alone should leave little doubt in your mind that the world cares a whole lot about creativity. And, while Robinson addresses his critical question to the traditional K-12 education system, we should also be asking ourselves what we're doing in early education to cultivate creativity during these critically formative years.

According to the American Psychological Association, creativity is formally defined as "the ability to produce or develop original work, theories, techniques, or thoughts"; it elaborates that "a creative individual typically displays originality, imagination, and expressiveness."[94] Beyond just the ability to produce something novel, it's also the usefulness or value of whatever creativity yields that matters. You'll also find that creativity is often grouped with a whole host of other desirable traits that, in addition to serving as keys to success in today's world, serve to define WHAT IF.

> 🚀 **WHAT IF Skills** are the possibility skills that allow us to understand not just how the world is, but envision how it could be. These skills are at the heart of innovation, imagination, ingenuity, creativity, originality, open-mindedness, out-of-the-box thinking, wonder, and hope.

What is WHAT IF?

WHAT IF Skills are a group of highly prized abilities that enable us to envision things in new and different ways from what currently exists. In other words, they allow us to think about, ask, and then act on the question, "What if?" WHAT IF is most obviously about creativity, but it's also much broader, as it is the WHAT IF Skills that allow children, and all of us, to look at the world through a lens of wonder, imagining what could be.

WHAT IF encompasses:

- Creativity
- Imagination
- Innovation
- Ingenuity
- Originality
- Open-mindedness
- Out-of-the-box thinking
- Wonder
- Hope

WHAT IF allows children to believe that not even the sky's the limit. Instead of operating within the framework of "You have to see it to believe it," WHAT IF is the ability to see opportunities and possibilities—not just problems—and believe that if you can imagine it, you just might be able to create or achieve it. As adults, we know this on a very instinctual level. What's so powerful about WHAT IF Skills is that they allow us to envision not only how our lives could be, but also the *world* as it could be.

We want children to grow up believing that they can be anything they want to be: a scientist, president, teacher, doctor, dancer, zookeeper, programmer, business owner, and, yes, some days even a superhero. With WHAT IF, we can imagine a better world. By drawing on all of the other QI Skills, we have the power to help children develop the skills necessary to transform their visions into realities.

WHY vs. WHAT IF

At this point in the QI Skill conversation, it often occurs to people that WHAT IF and WHY sound similar. Both, after all, are questions designed to probe for answers and generate new understanding. The best way I've found to differentiate these two QI Skills is to point out that while WHY involves asking questions about how the world works to better understand the way it *is*, WHAT IF involves questioning if it has to be that way, and imagining how it *could be*. In short, WHY Skills inform us and give us the building blocks we need to understand how the world works; WHAT IF Skills help us imagine what else we might create with those blocks.

DEVELOPING CREATIVE AND INNOVATIVE MINDS

Getting right to the heart of WHAT IF, esteemed Swiss developmental psychologist Jean Piaget asked, "Are we forming children who are only capable of learning that which is already known? Or should we try to develop creative and innovative minds, capable of discovery... throughout life?"[95] As I suggest throughout this chapter, the answer should ideally be the latter.

WHAT IF: It's who we are

The good news when it comes to cultivating children's creativity is that, as many would argue, this is central to who we are as human beings. In 2015, I had the opportunity to attend the Creativity World Forum, the annual event dedicated to advancing creative culture. Sir Ken Robinson was the featured speaker, and something he said about why we all should care so much about creativity really struck a chord. To paraphrase, he said that what defines us as humans isn't just our opposable thumbs, but our ability to imagine things that don't yet exist.[96] LinkedIn co-founder Reid Hoffman has similarly emphasized this sentiment, asserting that "the will to create is encoded in the human DNA."[97]

This ability to think creatively and innovate also happens to be wired into our brains. Rather than the outdated right brain (creative) versus left brain (analytical) model that's been shown to be oversimplified and inaccurate, what we now know is that everyone's brain has what has been described as an "innovation circuit." More formally referred to as the "default mode network," this is associated with mind-wandering and daydreaming, and it can't be fully accessed at the same time as the more task-oriented (executive function) circuitry in the brain. "That means the first thing you need to do to boost creativity is to deliberately turn off your analytical mind," explains Michael Platt, a neuroscience professor in the Wharton School at the University of Pennsylvania. "[We know] the brain is often at its most creative when it's not working on a specific problem."[98]

Although the WHAT IF–defining skills are not yet as easily measured as IQ, researchers are finding plenty of new and interesting ways (including brain imaging) to get a clearer picture of just when, where and how these abilities develop in children's brains. For example, with the help of books and brain scans, pediatric researchers in Cincinnati were able to take a closer look at the inner workings of imagination. What they found was that reading books to young children literally helps build up the part of the brain responsible for seeing things in the "mind's eye." Preschoolers whose parents reported reading books to them at home showed significantly greater activation of this part of the brain.[99] This and other brain research gives scientific reinforcement to the belief that reading aloud to young children not only plants the seeds of creativity, but also allows the roots of children's imagination to start taking hold.

Planting the seeds of innovation

If creativity and the ability to ask, imagine, and act on the question "What if?" are what make us human, and our brains come equipped with the dedicated circuitry to do so, then it stands to reason that the underlying WHAT IF Skills aren't necessarily something we need to teach young children, so much as they are inborn qualities that we need to nurture and protect.

Unfortunately, it can be all too easy in the traditional approach to education (and parenting) to unintentionally squelch children's innate curiosity and creativity. Psychologists even have a term for this process: *enculturation*. Enculturation refers to how, over time, we increasingly adhere to the status quo—i.e., what's culturally accepted and expected—and fall into routines that make life easier and simpler but that cause us to be less imaginative. We then pass this mentality on to our children, enculturating them from the time they're born. It's perfectly understandable how this happens, especially as these traits were central to traditional 20th-century education. It's not that we want children to be less creative or inquisitive; it's simply that we want them to be realistic, learn the rules, and master existing knowledge. But while our intentions in this may be good, the outcomes may not be. When we examine how a rigid focus on rule-following and established ways of doing things can serve to block children's developing WHAT IF Skills, it's clear that a rethinking of our approach is in order.

RECOGNIZING THE ROOTS OF INNOVATION

In describing how entrepreneurs create the world they envision, global business leader and serial entrepreneur Peter Diamandis makes clear that the innovation and creativity so critical in today's world of work have their origins in childhood. "Kids happen to be some of the most imaginative humans around," says Diamandis, adding that "it is critical that they know how important and liberating imagination can be."[100]

An important shift you can make in regard to WHAT IF Skills is to commit to creating a classroom culture that expressly embraces creativity (if yours doesn't already). We can start in our classrooms by distinguishing between situations that warrant direct answers, instructions or knowledge-sharing, and those opportunities that encourage children to practice asking, "What if?" To this end, I'm often reminded of a trip I took with my children to an art museum when my older son was five. As we stood in front of a very large and colorful abstract glass sculpture, he asked me, "What's that?" I nearly replied instinctively with an answer along the lines of, "It's a glass sculpture by a very famous artist named Dale Chihuly that kind of looks like colorful coral under the sea." But then I caught myself and replied, "What do you think it is?"

As early educators, we become quite good at answering a whole lot of questions. But by not always settling for the first answer that comes to mind, you have the potential to help set children's imaginations free. You can hand them the opportunity to discover that there's not always one right answer or approach to everything, that adults aren't all-knowing, and that there's often room for imagination, interpretation, and for asking the key (and QI!) question: "What if?"

LITTLE HANDS, BIG IMAGINARY FEATS

It's a typical spring afternoon. I walk into a classroom in my childcare center to find three pre-kindergarten students focused on an eclectic mix of toys that have been strategically placed in a pattern the significance of which is not exactly (or even remotely) clear to me. There is a box and a tower of wood blocks stacked almost as tall as those responsible for stacking them. As I attempt to step carefully across what might justifiably be perceived by some as one big mess, the architects of said "mess" implore me to proceed with caution, lest I find myself in grave danger.

I was, as it turned out, stepping into an imaginary world of spaceships and evil villains, where the daunting task of saving the planet rests squarely on the shoulders of pint-sized caped crusaders who stand united in their shared belief that they will not fail. This powerful, albeit messy, image of imaginative "make-believe" play is both cute and commonplace. But it's more than that: it also paints a picture of what it looks like to apply WE, WILL, WIGGLE and WOBBLE to the playful task of imagining the seemingly unimaginable and believing in endless possibilities—highly sought-after skills that, along with creativity and other related abilities, capture the very essence of WHAT IF.

The growth of creativity

As we finish this introduction to the final of the seven QI Skills, it's worth reinforcing that these skills are intricately interconnected and all serve to facilitate one another. That said, what makes WHAT IF unique is that, more than any other, it is the QI Skill that ties the rest of the individual skills together. Without ME, WE, WHY, WILL, WIGGLE and WOBBLE, it would be difficult, if not impossible, for children (or adults) to be creative, to innovate, or to conjure up fresh possibilities, much less have the skills or drive to act on them.

In other words, it's a strong sense of ME, combined with the collaborative foundation of WE and driven by motivational WILL, that allows children to ask WHY and WIGGLE their way through a world that embraces WOBBLE so they can learn to ask WHAT IF and create opportunities that will ultimately improve their lives and the world around them.

PUTTING WHAT IF TO WORK

It has been said that few things shape the human experience as profoundly or as pervasively as creativity, whether in the form of a creative person, process or product.[101] The value of this WHAT IF–defining concept is certainly not lost on today's business leaders, as evidenced by the following examples:

- According to the World Economic Forum's *Future of Jobs Report 2023*, creativity ranks second only to analytical thinking as a core skill. Also notably in the top 10 are resilience, flexibility and agility (WOBBLE); motivation (WILL); self-awareness (ME); and empathy and active listening (WE).[102]

- CEOs consistently reinforce the importance of creativity. In a global survey of more than 1,500 CEOs, creativity was identified as the most crucial factor for future success,[103] while in another, CEOs identified open-mindedness (along with curiosity) as increasingly critical in challenging times.[104]

- Richard Florida, a columnist for *The Atlantic* and acclaimed author of *The Rise of the Creative Class*, notes that "Access to talented and creative people is to modern business what access to coal and iron was to steel-making" in the Industrial Era.[105] Extrapolating this concept to childhood education, Virginia Heffernan in the *New York Times* asserts that "Creativity is the raw material that will enable today's [young children] to invent, fulfill and succeed in those careers that don't yet exist using the tools that have yet to be imagined."[106]

This growing recognition of creativity's importance makes good sense, and is good news for anyone in the business of cultivating young children's WHAT IF Skills—like you! In a world where facts and technology are at young children's (even toddlers') fingertips, it is WHAT IF–defining traits such as creativity and open-mindedness that will allow them to apply these facts in new, clever, and useful ways. Rather than just focusing on information, memorization and execution, the world has become all about imagination, creativity and innovation. And your dedication to the nurturing of young children's WHAT IF Skills is one of the most promising paths to get us there.

DEVELOPMENTAL MILESTONES
Make-believe milestones

Unlike the more predictable course of early childhood language development that serves to build WE Skills, or the motor milestones that facilitate WIGGLE, the timeline for milestones associated with WHAT IF Skills is a bit hazier. But that's not to say there aren't some easy-to-identify milestones, such as pretend play and the ability to understand that something that's hidden from sight still exists.

The following are examples of developmental milestones related to WHAT IF:

Milestones

Six months
Between four and seven months of age, infants begin to develop the concept of object permanence—the understanding that objects and people still exist even when they

can't be seen, heard, touched, smelled or otherwise sensed physically. While still falling somewhat into the category of WHY Skills (i.e., figuring out how the world works), the fact that infants are motivated to search for a toy hidden under a blanket or act on their newfound understanding that an object placed out of sight still exists serves as a visible, intriguing and fun precursor to imagining something can be brought into existence that isn't immediately in front of you.

Nine months

Peek-a-boo represents both a fun game and a classic nine-month milestone where babies demonstrate a clearer awareness that people and objects can still exist even when they can't be seen.

12 to 18 months

While during this period much emphasis is put on children learning to use objects in the ways they were designed to be used—from spoons and cups to brushes and combs—what you're also likely to see is toddlers starting to explore toys and objects in new, creative ways outside intended uses, such as shaking, banging and throwing them. By around 15 months, toddlers are likely to demonstrate what can be seen as a core building block for creating new things as they demonstrate their ability to stack at least two objects.

Two years

In addition to looking for and finding objects that are initially out of sight, two-year-olds engage in early forms of creative play, including pretend play. They may engage in simple make-believe games as they increasingly show interest in interactive play, and their imaginative play becomes more elaborate.

Three years

Preschoolers engage in role-play and fantasy play and may frequently switch back and forth between their imaginary worlds and reality. It's not uncommon for three-year-olds to have imaginary friends. Whereas the appearance of imaginary friends was once considered a potential cause for concern, it's now recognized to be a normal and creative aspect of social-emotional development for preschoolers and older children.

Four years

For four-year-olds, pretending to be someone (or something) else is the name of the game—from superheroes to teachers to a cat or dog. At this age, children enjoy exploring and doing new things in new ways rather than just sticking to the tried and true. They become even more creative with make-believe play. Role-playing and pretend play is considered so developmentally important that it actually warrants a visit to the pediatrician for evaluation if a child doesn't show interest in these forms of play. Children this age should be able to tell you what they think is going to happen next in a book they haven't read before, which indicates a move further into the realm of thinking about, predicting and anticipating the future (literally asking "Why?" followed by "What if?") rather than just operating within what's already known.

Five years

Kindergarteners become better at distinguishing between what's real and what's imaginary. The goal going forward should be to value both of these perspectives rather than discounting the world of make-believe in favor of existing facts and norms.

STAGE	WHAT IF MILESTONES
4–7 months	begin to understand that objects and people still exist even when they can't be seen, heard or touched
9 months	peek-a-boo
1–2 years	the start of pretend play, find creative new ways to use toys
3–5 years	actively engage in the world of make-believe, with greater imagination, imaginary friends, and the enhanced ability to engage in thinking about, predicting and anticipating the future

CLASSROOM QI-NNECTIONS
Making WHAT IF a reality

Like WHY and all of the other QI Skills, there is an aspect of WHAT IF that is innate. Even the youngest children naturally examine the bewildering and intriguing world they're in and start to ask, "what if?" It's up to us, then, to encourage them to continue asking and imagining. In today's complex and rapidly changing world, we need people who are skilled in more than following directions and rules: we need individuals who are masters of reinvention, who can dream up and bring to life ideas that no one ever imagined before.

While the traditional K-12 education system was Sir Ken Robinson's focus, we now know that it is in the early months and years of a child's life that creativity and WHAT IF Skills are born. Furthermore, it is during these earliest years when you, as an early educator, stand to play a key role in encouraging (and not squelching) these valuable skills. By successfully cultivating these all-important QI

Skills now, you can help ensure that your students will thrive well beyond the early childhood years of pretend, dress-up and make-believe. In a world that prizes vision, creation and innovation, you play a very valuable role.

Like many of the other QI Skills, the beauty of WHAT IF is that young children naturally thrive in a WHAT IF world. Given a supportive environment in which their imaginations can run free, you'll find they're eager to creatively explore, question and play in ways that strengthen the foundations of this crucial set of skills. In many ways, your job can be made both easier and you can be more supportive by simply creating the time, space, and opportunities children need to move away from step-by-step instructions and predetermined rules to think, play and explore in new ways. Below are some strategies you can apply to encourage WHAT IF Skills development.

"I believe passionately that we don't grow into creativity, we grow out of it; or rather, we get educated out of it."[107]

SIR KEN ROBINSON

Activities

- **Read all about it**. Enjoy shared reading time as much, as early, and as often as you can. Reading remains one of the most powerful tools for cultivating WHAT IF (and all other QI Skills) for countless reasons, not the least of which is that it fosters children's ability to imagine things that don't actually exist and picture new worlds in their mind's eye. Some highly creative authors such as Peter

Reynolds (in his *Creatrilogy* consisting of *Dot, Ish* and *Sky Color*) capture the essence of WHAT IF particularly well.

- **Offer open-ended toys.** Fostering outside-the-box thinking is difficult to do when so many toys and games are designed to be used in very specific, predetermined ways that leave little to nothing up to a child's imagination. While following rules and instructions can be valuable for the development of ME and WE Skills, it's important to allow children to play games and play with toys that can be used in more creative and imaginative ways, and to encourage them to make up their own games. Some examples of fun, open-ended toys include blocks, playdough, dress-up clothes and props, kitchen sets and art supplies. Don't forget that young children can use even basic objects to discover new, interesting ways to play. Witness the classic example of young children enjoying playing with a cardboard box as much—if not more—than the toy that was in it.

A BALANCING ACT BETWEEN STRUCTURE AND CREATIVE FREEDOM

Asked how teachers can best balance the need for a structured learning environment while at the same time allowing for original thinkers to thrive, Wharton business school professor and best-selling author Adam Grant points out that "too much structure, order, and discipline can constrain [children's] creativity, but so can too little."

He suggests what it takes to get it just right—achieving the right balance between structure, order and discipline on the one hand and creative freedom on the other (in other words, the Goldilocks principle)—is a good understanding of child development, a clear picture of your ultimate goals, and, of course, a bit of finesse.

- **Praise ideas**. Whether they're goofy or genius, show children that you value their original ideas. Try to create a classroom atmosphere in which thinking up and sharing new ideas is encouraged, no matter how silly or outlandish they might seem. When possible, entertain children's ideas: help them describe, draw, or design and build the objects they imagine using a range of classroom items or supplies, and ask them to elaborate on how they might go about carrying out or bringing to life one of their ideas.

- **Support make-believe**. Encouraging children's make-believe and pretend play can serve as a simple and highly effective way to make sure they get the chance to regularly engage their WHAT IF Skills in your classroom. Having some dress-up clothes or offering a simple prompt or themed suggestion can help unleash their imaginations. Make-believe play, like pretending to be someone else and engaging with others within the structure of an imagined world, exercises not only WHAT IF Skills but also ME Skills (following rules and controlling one's emotions) and WE Skills (communication and collaboration), while also doing wonders for enhancing WILL.

THE POWER OF MAKE BELIEVE

Researchers have extensively studied the role of pre-tend play in child development and have found that early imaginative play is associated with increased creative performance years later. Research on notably creative individuals, including Nobel Prize winners and MacArthur Foundation "genius grant" awardees, indicates that these highly accomplished individuals were more likely to have played make-believe and other imaginative games when they were young than others in their fields.[108]

- **Play along**. When children play pretend games or tell made-up stories, you can further encourage them by asking them to elaborate. For example, suggest an idea about a pretend scenario or make-believe role that you know is likely to be appealing or relevant to what you've been learning about in class or to something that's going on in their lives. Then, stand back and watch their imaginations grow. If your students ask you to play a part, have fun joining in if you like, but remember to keep your role a supportive one rather than taking the lead. Provide just enough engagement, suggestions or props to move their fantasy forward, but allow them to hone their WHAT IF Skills and run the show.

- **Ask thought-provoking questions**. Make it a point to ask lots of open-ended questions that elicit creative answers. Although questions with definitive answers are important for helping young children build their WHY Skills and knowledge base, asking what they think, how they feel, or what could happen in any given scenario will tap their growing vocabulary and imagination and boost their other WHAT IF Skills.

- **Tell stories.** Engage your own WHAT IF Skills by making up fanciful stories as a way to model and encourage young children's imagination. If this isn't exactly second nature for you, start by selecting a topic based on your students' interests—bugs, animals, fairies, trucks, superheroes, or pretty much anything, really. For my son who loved elephants, I might talk about a recent trip to the zoo, then use what he knew and had actually experienced as a starting point for what happened next in my elephant tale that was fanciful, made up, unlikely or silly. The younger children are, the more it will fall on you to keep the imaginative storyline going. As they get older (starting at age four or five, and sometimes younger), encourage them to run with the story themselves while you play along. Ask questions to keep the story going and unleash their creative potential.

- **Unplug**. A certain amount of exposure to developmentally appropriate electronic toys and digital technologies can be useful. Too much, however, has the very concerning potential to sap children's motivation to engage in WHAT IF activities, since open-ended play, boredom, and meaningful meandering have become all-too-infrequent occurrences in today's electronic universe. Many electronic toys are prescriptive: they require spelled-out behaviors or actions to function instead of allowing a child's imagination to take over.

> ## ONLINE VS. OFFLINE: TOY-RELATED TOUCHPOINTS
>
> Children and their caregivers have been shown to interact with electronic toys much differently than they do with traditional toys like blocks and books. Babies vocalize less, their parents speak fewer words, and the nature of their interaction is significantly different. Additionally, caregivers are more likely to give behavioral-related cues such as "do this" or "press that" than ask broader WHAT IF questions relevant to the context.[109]

- **Take the path less traveled.** Making a change as simple as taking a different route when walking outside, exploring a garden, or going on a new nature walk can open up a world of possibilities for you and your students to turn WHAT IF into no-cost, real-world action. Although there's value in maintaining routines (for us and for children), sometimes we unintentionally fall into the habit of doing the same things the same way, every day. In so doing, we limit opportunities for our children's brains to meander as they imagine and explore.

- **Question your rules.** Think twice before insisting that things must always be done in a certain way or that all rules must always be followed. Yes, rule following is an important skill to master, and legitimate safety concerns (and well-thought-out safety-related rules) should always come first. But, as an early educator, you also need to consider whether the many rules of early childhood truly serve important purposes. If a child wants to climb up a slide instead of sliding down it (when there's no one else at the top about to come down, of course) or to take apart or try out a new and different way of using a particular toy, don't automatically put your foot down. Instead, consider how questioning certain rules and norms allows children to think freely and exercise their developing WHAT IF Skills.

ENCOURAGING CREATIVITY IN YOUR CLASSROOM

According to the Cambridge Dictionary, creativity is "the ability to produce or use original and unusual ideas." As you think about applying this understanding to how you approach cultivating WHAT IF, pay particular attention to the words "original" and "unusual." Help children come up with, test out, and play with their own ideas, rather than just yours and those in the curriculum. Also, make sure to heed the cautionary note that follows the dictionary definition: "too many rules might deaden creativity."[110]

- **Color outside the lines**. Doing arts and crafts is a potentially great way for children to explore their imagination and creativity. While learning to color inside the lines serves many useful purposes (including developing fine motor skills and helping kids learn how to listen to and follow directions), be sure to give them as much time to color *outside* the lines—and to create their own lines.

Provide young children with age-appropriate art supplies, instruction and supervision, while also allowing
them to create something that doesn't already exist in
someone else's mind. In this regard, I am reminded of the
daily art activities we offered at the educational childcare center I used to own. Every now and then I needed
to gently remind a teacher that I'd far rather walk by a
board displaying toddler and preschool art projects and
not have it be picture perfect than see a dozen identi-
cal bunnies with every cotton-ball tail glued perfectly in
place. As nice and neat as these sorts of displays might
seem at first glance, all too often they reflect children's
ability to follow directions rather than giving evidence
of their innate creativity. To gain insights into children's
early creative expression, also take the opportunity to
have them describe to you what they've created. There's
no doubt that some of their answers will surprise and
impress you—and their parents, too, if you remember to
write them on the back of their artwork.

THE BUILDING BLOCKS OF CREATIVITY

Renowned neuroscientist Adele Diamond asserts that the
ability to disassemble and recombine elements in new
ways is the essence of creativity.[111]

- **Let them be bored—in the name of fostering creativity.**
Okay, so I realize that it's unrealistic to think that all parents will accept, much less embrace, the notion that part

of your job as an early educator is to bore their children. But it's worth noting that being bored has a way of allowing creative ideas to arise, while going from one formal activity to the next all day leaves no time for this kind of WHAT IF engagement. Allowing young children time to engage in more open-ended, less well-defined activities, as well as factoring in ample free time, enables them to explore their interests, what they've learned, and engage in more WHAT IF ways of thinking.

THE TIME FOR CREATIVITY

As neuropsychologist and creativity researcher Rex Jung has said, "If you're constantly in knowledge acquisition mode, there's not that quiet time to put it together... You have to have the raw materials in place... but you also have to have the time to put them together."[112]

- **Leave something to their imaginations**. While the long-standing perception in education that teachers just need to teach and children just need to listen is generally flawed, it is especially so when it comes to the nurturing of WHAT IF Skills. Rather than providing direct instruction, your goal in nurturing creative thought is to be sure to leave plenty of things up to children's imaginations. In supporting guided play, for example, feel free to offer up ideas or questions that encourage children to use their imagination, and then let them take it from there.

QI TAKEAWAYS: WHAT IF

- Whereas WHY Skills involve asking all sorts of questions to better understand how the world works, WHAT IF Skills allow us to understand not just how the world *is*, but envision how it *could be*.

- While WHY Skills give us the building blocks of understanding that we need to figure out how the world works, WHAT IF Skills help us imagine what new, novel things we can create with those blocks.

- It's a strong sense of ME, combined with the collaborative foundation of WE and WILL's motivational drive, that allows children to ask WHY, WIGGLE their way through a world that embraces WOBBLE, and ultimately put their WHAT IF Skills to good use.

- Even beyond wonder, creativity, originality, ingenuity, imagination and innovation, WHAT IF Skills represent hope and our ability to imagine a world or circumstance that's better than the one we are born into or currently facing.

QI REFLECTIONS: WHAT IF

- What are some things you do (or could do) in your classroom over the course of a typical day that help to encourage your students' imaginations and creativity?

- Think about each aspect of your daily routine, from circle time to snack or lunchtime, outdoor and free play to reading aloud and rest time. Now recall as many instances from a single day as you can when children in your class did something new, different, original or creative that involved out-of-the-box thinking and used their imaginations. What were the circumstances that allowed them to think creatively and play imaginatively? How involved were you? If you find that there are times in your daily routine for which you were unable to think of any examples, consider how you might encourage WHAT IF Skill development during these times.

- Make a list of things you do on a typical day. Actively consider which "network" you engage in your brain to accomplish these things: the more creative, "innovation" network, or your "task circuit"? How might you find ways and time in your day to step away from some analytical tasks to give your brain a creativity boost?

- Reflect for a moment on whether you consider yourself a creative person. What opportunities do you have—both at work and outside of work—to be creative? What is something you do, or have done, that was creative or required imagination. What were the circumstances that allowed you to do it? What did you need in the way of support, supplies, or setting to engage your WHAT IF Skills?

PART 2

QI SKILLS IN ACTION

OUR FOCUS thus far has been on getting to know each individual QI Skill, along with some ideas for how you might support development of each of these key skills. Now I want to go further to give you a better sense of just how easy it is for you to put QI Skills into action in the "real world" that is your classroom. Using the examples of play, belonging, behavioral challenges and everyday classroom routines, I'll illustrate how interrelated, relevant and useful QI Skills can be.

Let's start with one of the hottest topics of the day: play.

PLAYING IS QI

. . . .

"Play is the highest expression of
human development in childhood."

FRIEDRICH FROEBEL
father of kindergarten

"Children already know play is their superpower.
We're here to convince the grown-ups."

THE LEGO FOUNDATION

G IVEN THAT the goal of this book and the QI Skills
framework is to offer you a new lens through which
the foundational value of even the most routine
early childhood activities and interactions becomes clear, it
seems only fitting to start with play.

Of course, I am fully aware that many of you may justifiably consider yourself well-versed in play. After all, your role
as an early educator makes it highly likely that you come
to this discussion with more daily, up-close-and-personal,
hands-on experience planning for, observing, facilitating
and even partaking in play than most. That said, the goal
of this chapter is not to "school" you on play, nor to provide
an exhaustive review of all the evidence that reinforces the
essential nature of play and its impact on young children's
well-being, learning and development. Rather, it's meant to

reinforce the many recognized benefits of play through your new QI Skills lens. So let's take just a few moments to roll up our sleeves and play around with the QI Skills in action as we explore what play is (and isn't), what it represents, and the opportunities and obstacles involved in embracing play-as-learning in your classroom specifically in a QI Skill context. As you shall soon see, play serves as both a literal and figurative playground for the QI Skills.

The universal right to play

Play is a universal activity that, like the concept of *qi*, has been enjoyed across cultures, continents and centuries. While partaking in play and playful activities has, like the QI Skills, proven to be valuable at all ages, for our purposes we're going to stick to the globally recognized importance of play in early childhood. Understood to be at the center of the lives of all young children and their optimal development, play was formally recognized more than 30 years ago by the United Nations as a universal right of every child—ranking right up there with protection, education, health care, shelter and good nutrition.[113] As such, increasingly intentional efforts to support and validate play can be seen around the world.

THE GLOBAL STATE OF PLAY

Understood to be at the center of the lives of all young children, the value of play was globally established when it was formally recognized in 1989 by the United Nations Convention on the Rights of the Child as a universal right for every child.[114] How much value, you ask? Enough value for play to warrant being added to a critical list of previously declared rights of children that includes such basic human needs as health, education, shelter, protection, and nutrition. Given that the UN's Convention on the Rights of the Child is credited with having changed the way children are viewed and treated (as distinct human beings with rights), and is said to be the most rapidly and widely ratified international human rights treaty in history,[115] that's saying a lot for play!

Redefining play

For some, play is just play. For others, including early education professionals, play is comprised of a range of categories and based on a variety of features, from who's in charge (child-initiated, teacher-directed, free, guided) and who's involved (independent, parallel, interactive) to the type of play (active, imaginary or pretend) or location in which it takes place (outdoors, indoors). Given the universality of play in all its various forms, as well as the fact that just about everyone has played, it's understandable that everyone thinks they know play. What seems to be less than universal, however, is a contemporary understanding of just how valuable play actually is, much less the full breadth of its benefits, which extend well beyond the common perception of play as being nothing more than just "fun and games." Common definitions of play often fail to recognize its significance for development, including cultivating QI Skills.

....

"No single definition or cultural perspective
is sufficient to capture the richness of play...
A useful way of understanding play is that [it]
is both a process and a context for learning."

EARLY CHILDHOOD AUSTRALIA
Statement on Play (2023)

....

The following definitions are representative of what you might find should you google the word "play."

- A range of intrinsically motivated activities done for recreational pleasure and enjoyment.

- To engage in activity for enjoyment and recreation rather than a serious or practical purpose.

- To do things for pleasure, as children do; to enjoy yourself, rather than work.[116]

- To exercise or employ oneself in diversion, amusement or recreation or to do something in sport that is not to be taken seriously.[117]

- Synonym: recreational activity (especially the spontaneous activity of children).[118]

- Play is imaginative, intrinsically motivated, non-serious, freely chosen, and actively engaging.[119]

- Play is not neatly defined in terms of any single characteristic; instead, it involves a constellation of characteristics. The five most agreed-upon characteristics of human play are that it is (1) self-chosen and self-directed, (2) intrinsically motivated, (3) guided by mental rules, (4) imaginative, and (5) conducted in an active, alert, but relatively non-stressed frame of mind.[120]

As spelled out in the above definitions, play is often self-directed, guided by mental rules, and involves doing what one wants (ME), is intrinsically motivated (WILL), imaginative (WHAT IF), and actively engaging (WIGGLE, as well as the added benefits of the WHY, WILL and WOBBLE that often result from participating in engaging activities). That is, of course, in addition to all of the social interaction (WE) and the overcoming of challenges (WOBBLE) that are also common components of play. In short, play is integral to developing all of the QI Skills, offering children an entertaining, enjoyable and engaging context in which their QI Skills can play out and come to life.

WHAT IS PLAY IF NOT FUN?

It doesn't take a lot of deep thought or research to come to the conclusion that play, pretty much by definition, is meant to be fun. So, what happens when you take the fun out of play? In a very real-world sense, one only has to look at the way in which some organized, competitive sports have moved down into early childhood. Too often, this involves imposing strict rules and prioritizing competition over collaboration, with little to no regard for all of the QI Skill–related benefits that play has to offer.

Fun happens to be a great way to engage not just children, but people of all ages. Take away the fun and you run the risk of taking away the interest, engagement, and motivation that comes with it. In other words, it takes the WILL out of play—a serious concern given that intrinsic motivation is, after all, a defining feature of play.

Of course, then there are the definitional aspects of play that not-so-subtly imply that it's lacking in educational value. Fun, yes, but *not to be taken seriously*. A *diversion,* something done *for recreational pleasure and enjoyment rather than serious or practical purpose*. Alongside these definitional aspects, culturally accepted concepts such as "it's all work and no play" suggest that the two are direct opposites, and unrelated.

"[Play] is not a peripheral sideline to the serious job of adults and children at school. It does not simply provide a spontaneous interlude to the more structured work of the classroom."[121]

B. SPARROW

Our culture has long led us to believe that play serves no practical purpose, erroneously suggesting that it's not to be taken seriously. In other words, play is the opposite of work. It's what children do when they need a break from the work of learning and "formal" education.

What's now clearer than ever, however, is that serious learning can and does take place when children engage in play. Furthermore, while play has long been defined as being spontaneous, we know that playful learning can be both intentionally and strategically planned. Rather than drawing a rigid dividing line between work and play, we now have every reason (not to mention a whole lot of evidence) to support the understanding that play *is* learning. Play is important not only for "three Rs"–type learning (the IQ Skills), but the practice, nurturing, and cultivation of all of the equally valuable QI Skills as well.

NOT JUST CHILD'S PLAY, BUT SERIOUS BUSINESS

Children aren't the only ones naturally drawn to play. People of all ages, as well as many "higher-functioning animals"—from birds to other mammals—participate in playful activities. Although play is increasingly being recognized as the "work" of young children, when it comes to the development of skills that support lifelong success, including in our professional lives, we'd be wise to acknowledge that work really should be more like the play of young children!

Learning to play, playing to learn

For children, play is a seriously effective superpower. Not only is it essential for their healthy growth and development, it also allows them to learn all sorts of valuable things about the world and themselves. How children play evolves over time, and contributes to everything from cognitive and physical development to their ability to self-regulate and their social and emotional well-being.[122] In fact, simply watching young children play can provide you with a whole lot of insights about how both they and their QI Skills are developing.

THE IMPORTANCE OF PLAY FOR
HEALTHY DEVELOPMENT

In 2007, the American Academy of Pediatrics released a report that clearly identified play as "essential to the cognitive, physical, social, and emotional well-being of children" and formally voiced concern that "hurried life-style[s] as well as an increased focus on the fundamentals of academic preparation in lieu of a broader view of education" was negatively impacting and limiting children's access to play. Citing the many benefits of play—from healthy brain development to dexterity to the development of creativity, confidence and conflict resolution—the AAP declared it "imperative that play be included along with academic and social-enrichment opportunities and that safe [play] environments be made available to all children."[123]

Developmental milestones of play

Since play provides such a valuable opportunity for QI Skill cultivation and development, it only makes sense to review some of the play-related developmental milestones of early childhood (which you may recall having seen earlier in specific QI Skill chapters).

Milestones

Four months
Four-month-olds enjoy interacting and playing with others and respond to affection with smiles and coos.

12 months
As children round out their first year they become increasingly social, playing interactive games like pat-a-cake and waving bye-bye.

Two-and-a-half to three years
Whereas prior to this age children tend to engage mostly in "parallel" play, now is when they may choose to play *with* other children, rather than just alongside them. This represents a significantly more social and interactive shift in the way they interact and play.

Four years
At this age, children typically become less "me-centric," as evidenced by their newfound preference for playing, cooperating and sharing with other children rather than simply playing next to them. They're also becoming more adept at perspective-taking with dress-up and make-believe play. Interactive games tend to be especially appealing to most four-year-olds, who would often rather play with others than by themselves.

QI aspects of play

Play, in all its many forms, serves as a one-stop shop when it comes to recognizing, supporting, exercising and generally cultivating QI Skills. To help illustrate this link, here are some benefits of play highlighted in Early Childhood Australia's 2023 "Statement on Play." Take a look at each and think about, write down or discuss with a colleague which QI Skills come into play with each.

- "Play builds each child's capacity for communication and develops language and thinking skills."

- "Through play, young children develop a sense of self and the emotional and social competence to participate in relationships."

- "Play connects children to their world, their cultural identities, to others and to other ways of knowing, doing and being."

- "While ideas about play often emphasize fun, play can encompass risk, challenge, problem-solving, self-awareness and conflict resolution."

- "Play is both a process and a context for learning; an experience of activity freely engaged in, where the child makes decisions, learns from their experiences, solves difficulties, and may have fun and take risks."

- "All children in every culture and setting play as a way of interacting with and learning about their world and understanding who they are in relation to others."

While the list below is by no means exhaustive, here are some of the QI Skills that relate to each of the above statements:

- WE
- ME and WE
- ME, WE and WHY
- ME, WE, WHY, WILL and WOBBLE
- ME, WHY, WILL, WIGGLE and WOBBLE
- ME, WE, WHY and WIGGLE

Now, consider a couple of the play-related conclusions drawn from the book *The Play's the Thing:*

- "To play requires great flexibility in thinking, an ability to shift context and to add new ideas. These skills, which will be useful across an entire life cycle, do not come without practice."[124]

- "Play is intrinsically motivating, and children voluntarily relinquish impulsive behaviors and immediate gratification to align their actions to the unfolding script. In play, children are active agents who reflect on and coordinate their own thoughts, rather than merely absorbing those of others."[125]

Hopefully, the mention of flexibility in thinking, shifting context, and the ability to take in and respond to new ideas remind you of the executive function skills we discussed earlier—skills that figure prominently in the ME Skills—with the reference to new ideas also potentially leading you to see budding WHAT IF Skills. As for play motivating children to control their impulsive behaviors, delay gratification and follow the rules, you can likely now see the WILL and the ME behind those choices.

Here's where, based on a sampling of play-related research, other aspects of play intuitively fit into the QI Skills framework (understanding that many relate to multiple skillsets):

ME

- "Through games and playful activities, children can practice and strengthen important executive function skills that will help them throughout their lives, including learning to focus their attention, strengthening their working memory, and developing basic self-control."[126]

- When engaged in play, "children voluntarily relinquish impulsive behaviors and immediate gratification to align their actions to the unfolding script."[127]

♥ WE

- Play helps children work out the rules for social interaction.

- "In self-directed play young children practice empathy—learning sensitivity to one another's emotions and intentions."[128]

❓ WHY

- "Play is children's first language for making meaning of the world."[129]

- "All children in every culture and setting play as a way of interacting with and learning about their world, and understanding who they are in relation to others."[130]

⬆ WILL

- Nothing enhances WILL like fun, engaging, recreational pleasure and enjoyment.

- Play is, by definition, intrinsically motivating.

〰 WIGGLE

- "Children learn best in active, playful learning."[131]

- "Play… begins as exploration of the physical world… young children learn not by being told but by constructing knowledge through actions with objects in the real world."[132]

- Play provides "time to find and make connections between personal, hands-on experience and 'the outside world with its rules, expectations and conventions.'"[133]

- "All children in every culture and setting play as a way of interacting with and learning about their world."[134]

WOBBLE

- "While ideas about play often emphasize fun, play can encompass risk, challenge, problem-solving... and conflict resolution."[135]

- "Play is both a process and a context for learning; an experience... where the child makes decisions, learns from their experiences, solves difficulties, and may... take risks."[136]

WHAT IF

- "Play is free from many of the constraints of objective reality."[137]

- "Play is free-flowing fun that unleashes our imagination."[138]

- "In their play, children invent the world and create a place for themselves in it. They are re-creating their pasts and imagining their futures while grounding themselves in the reality and fantasy of their lives here and now."[139]

QI TAKEAWAYS: PLAY

- Play is essential to all children's healthy growth and development, including the development of QI Skills.

- There are many types of play that allow children to actively engage and develop their QI Skills.

- Play serves as a literal and figurative playground for the QI Skills.

- By definition, being playful may mean not being too serious, but that doesn't mean the benefits of play—and the need for it—shouldn't be taken seriously.

- If nothing else, what we've learned about play is that it's critical for learning. This is especially true when it comes to honing QI Skills.

- Rarely does a task, concept or activity apply to or represent a single QI Skill. Rather, any given activity has the potential to capture, cultivate or represent several if not all of the QI Skills.

QI REFLECTIONS: PLAY

- Think about your approach to play. Without judgment, ask yourself whether you see and treat play as a valuable opportunity for learning, or more as a break from learning?

- Write down a few specific examples of when children in your classroom engage in play on any given day. Try to identify all the QI Skills that are involved. Then, working with a colleague, see if you can come up with new ways to support your students' development of QI Skills through play.

- Think about what it means to be playful. How often are you playful? How might you be more playful, and how do you think this would impact your effectiveness as a teacher? When does it make more sense to be more straightforward or serious? How do children react when you're playful?

THE QI TO
BELONGING

· · · · · · · · · · · · · · · · · · ·

"To belong is to matter."[140]

NATHANIEL M. LAMBERT ET AL

Personality and Social Psychology Bulletin

O
UR NEXT TOPIC is belonging—which, like play, has
increasingly been a subject of considerable interest
in early education, and beyond. As with play, belonging (often interchangeably referred to as belongingness) also
happens to be well-suited to being better understood, not to
mention cultivated, through a QI Skills lens.

QI aspects of belonging

As with play, taking a look at the definition of belonging
quickly proves itself to be a useful exercise. In the case
of belonging, however, it's not so much because everyone
thinks they already know all about it; rather, it's because
it can be a bit challenging to actually put one's finger on
exactly what it is, and why it seems to have all of a sudden
become such a hot topic of discussion.

Let's start by simply considering a handful of common
definitions and descriptions of belonging (or belongingness).

In addition to serving as a useful starting point and making sure we're all on the same page, the following definitions also serve to make it all the more obvious how belonging(ness) is both supported by and, in turn, supports the QI Skills.

- A noun that refers to "the feeling of being accepted and approved by a group or by society as a whole."[141]

- "A sense of fitting in or feeling like you are an important member of a group."[142]

- "A feeling of being happy or comfortable as part of a particular group and having a good relationship with the other members of the group because they welcome you and accept you."[143]

- "The quality or state of being an essential or important part of something."[144]

What hopefully jumps out as you read these definitions is that belongingness has a whole lot to do with the sense of self and identity that characterize inward-facing aspects of ME. Belonging also, by definition, has everything to do with the more outward-facing features of WE, given that it's all about how one interacts with and feels in relation to others. In fact, it is a combination of ME and WE Skills that, in a general sense, serve as the foundation for building the "culture of belonging" so frequently discussed and so highly sought after in classrooms, communities and corporations alike.

GETTING TO US

Belongingness is defined by a feeling of being a part of "us"—of fitting in and being accepted as part of a group or community. ME and WE can be seen as the individual QI Skills that, when nurtured and applied in group settings, allow for the highly sought-after feeling of belonging and the collective culture of belongingness. In other words, a culture of "us."

Factoring belongingness into a really simple QI Skill equation, it might look something like this:

ME + WE = US

Of course, while ME and WE serve as necessary ingredients for cultivating a culture of belonging, one need only look at the classic pyramid representing Maslow's Hierarchy of Needs to see that there's more to the relationship between belongingness and the QI Skills than just a dependence on ME and WE. This pyramid, depicting the developmental theory of human motivation, highlights the essential needs we all have as humans.

While it may seem like belongingness has only recently entered the mainstream of discussion about early childhood education, in reality its importance has long been recognized. Referring back to Maslow's Hierarchy of Needs, which was first introduced in 1943 by American psychologist Abraham Maslow,[145] you'll find belonging at the very center level of this hierarchy, sitting right alongside love.

Belonging as a QI cultivation strategy

The best way to think about belonging's relationship to QI Skills is to understand that the efforts you make to nurture ME and WE Skills in your classroom contribute to creating a feeling of belonging. In turn, a climate of belonging not only helps strengthen engagement and motivation (WILL), but also provides the conditions necessary for children to exercise all of their other QI Skills. So, how exactly does one cultivate a sense of belonging? Let's take a look at some belongingness "best practices" below.

1   Spend time listening.

2   Spend time learning how to talk in ways that facilitate better communication with others who are different from you.

3   Create intentional connections, thinking about how groups can be brought together to solve specific problems.

4   Invite opinions and perspectives into the conversation.

5   Amplify everyone's voices.

6   Appreciate others for their unique backgrounds.

7   Engage in purposeful storytelling and encourage everyone to share their individual stories. This helps to highlight the many layers, dimensions and experiences of others. In short, when we share our story, we feel seen.

This list—which sounds a whole lot like a description of a warm, inviting, thoughtfully run early childhood classroom— was actually derived from business literature. Unsurprisingly, it reads like a list of ME- and WE-cultivating activities. Active listening, for example, requires both ME Skills (controlling one's impulse to talk in order to be a good listener) and WE Skills, where listening is core to under-standing, communicating, and interacting with others, and, of course, in making them feel heard.

QI TAKEAWAYS: BELONGING

- The recognition of belonging's foundational importance is not new, dating all the way back to the creation of Maslow's original Hierarchy of Needs pyramid depicting the developmental theory of human motivation.

- Belonging(ness) represents a good example of how it's not just the cultivation of QI Skills that matters, but also creating the culture and environment in which QI Skill development is best nurtured and supported.

- ME and WE are valuable skills for creating a culture of belonging. In turn, a culture of belonging plays a foundational role in supporting the development of all of the QI Skills.

QI REFLECTIONS: BELONGING

- Take a moment to reflect on a typical day in your classroom. What things do you routinely say, do, introduce or facilitate that help all children feel like they belong? See if you can identify specific ways in which your efforts to create a culture of belonging rely on or support their QI Skill development.

- Consider a situation, environment, or group where you felt you truly belonged. What was it that made you feel that way? What did this feeling do for your motivation? Your curiosity? Your willingness to get your hands dirty, try new things, and make (and learn from) your mistakes? Your ability to be creative? In other words, what impact do you think the feeling of belongingness has had in supporting your own QI Skill development?

SEEING THE QI
IN CHALLENGING
BEHAVIORS

*"When adults reframe perceptions about
children they perceive as difficult, it is possible to
positively transform the teacher-child relationship."*[146]

**ADDRESSING CHALLENGING BEHAVIORS
IN EARLY CHILDHOOD SETTINGS**

*"When we don't understand a behavior,
we tend to assume a child is doing it on purpose."*[147]

PREVENT-TEACH-REINFORCE FOR FAMILIES

NEXT UP in our discussion of QI Skills in action is
a quick, QI-framed consideration of some of the
challenging behaviors commonly seen in the early
childhood classroom—a look that will involve a slightly different approach than we've taken thus far. In contrast to
play, where we recognized ways in which the QI Skills factor
in and can be strengthened, or belonging(ness), where we
established how QI Skills foundationally support and are
supported by this feeling, we're now going to focus on simply helping you see the QI in behaviors that are commonly
viewed as disruptive to learning. This is a QI strategy that's

ultimately intended to make it easier for you to understand and feel confident in your ability to manage your classroom.

It's worth noting that effectively addressing any particular behavioral challenge generally involves taking into consideration all sorts of additional information, including specific details about each child involved, not to mention such relevant factors as the environment, circumstances, timing and frequency of the behavior. Responding to and resolving challenging behaviors also tends to take time, a lot of caring support and, more often than not, some trial and error. While entire books and courses have been written on this subject, the goal here is to provide you with a general, QI-based strategy that you can use to assess, address and accommodate (or adjust) these challenging behaviors in a developmentally appropriate and QI-informed way.

Seeing the ME

Let's jump right in by considering how QI Skills might play a useful role in assessing the following list of common challenging preschool behaviors you've likely experienced many times in your classroom:[148]

- Biting
- Temper tantrums
- Hitting
- Talking out of turn
- Screaming
- Refusing to cooperate
- Throwing toys or other objects
- Lashing out

While these are behaviors with which you are undoubtedly quite familiar, I want you to take another look at the list above. This time, ask yourself the additional question, "Is there something underlying each of these behaviors that they all have in common?" The answer, as you might suspect, is "yes."

What each of these behaviors has in common is a distinct lack of self-control—in other words, a lack of the ME-defining ability to be in control of one's own thoughts, feelings or actions. As you'll recall from the ME Skills chapter, young children don't demonstrate much in the way of self-control (one of the three defining features of the ME-related executive function skills) until between the ages of three to five. This QI developmental insight means that in any early childhood classroom—be it infant, toddler, preschool or pre-kindergarten—ME Skills should be viewed as a work in progress to be practiced and encouraged, but not expected.

WHAT DO YOU EXPECT FROM ME?

Developmentally appropriate practice inherently involves developmentally appropriate QI expectations. Based on all we know about ME Skills and the developmental course of self-control, for example, expecting young children to dependably refrain from hitting, throwing, having a temper tantrum, biting or engaging in any other of the common lack-of-self-control behaviors is as unrealistic as expecting toddlers to be able to tie their own shoes.

In addition to considering what can be expected with respect to QI Skill development at any given age, as with any aspect of learning it's also worth noting that lots of other things—from lack of sleep, to illness, to emotional upset—can make it more challenging for young children to put their budding ME Skills into practice.

While ME Skills (or lack thereof) are at the core of many of the most common behavioral challenges, it's also worth thinking about these challenges from a WE perspective. Whenever you refrain from lashing out, screaming or hitting, you're certainly engaging your ME Skills. But you are also driven to do so, in large part, because of your WE Skills. After all, WE Skills are what allow you to consider how your actions might affect others and how they will likely make others feel. Of course, WE Skills, like ME Skills, take time to develop. One's ability to stop short of acting on these impulses (ME) is, in part, dependent on one's ability to consider the perspective of those who might be affected by such behaviors.

QI responses to challenging behaviors

Different kinds of challenging behaviors call for different responses that take into account the full range of QI Skills. To better understand how these might be applied, it's helpful to consider various real-world examples. A child who interrupts might be viewed as lacking in ME and WE Skills, while at the same time demonstrating an abundance of engagement (WILL) and curiosity (WHY). A child who doesn't follow rules or uses objects in ways other than instructed may well pose a challenge while at the same time be exercising their creativity (WHAT IF).

The following represent actual questions I've been asked about challenging behaviors in the early childhood classroom. Each is meant to serve as an example of how you can apply a QI lens to better understand not only how to address challenging behaviors, but to see them for what they are.

❓ What's the best way to keep a very energetic child busy?

To me, this common "challenge" actually represents a great WIGGLE opportunity. Not only does coming up with ways for children to more actively participate in hands-on learning tend to enhance their engagement and learning, but for energetic children in particular, it's also usually a whole lot easier than trying to make them sit still. As a bonus, you can engage your own WHAT IF Skills by coming up with creative offerings.

❓ What's the best way to address a lack of focus in the classroom?

The most obvious first QI Skill that comes to mind is ME, given that focus and attention serve to define ME and, of course, take time to develop. Additionally, however, it's worth considering that a perceived lack of focus might also be related to a problematic lack of interest in what's being presented or how it's being presented. Are there ways you might introduce more hands-on (WIGGLE) activities related to what you're attempting to teach? Or, consider finding additional ways to relate the subject at hand to something the children are already interested in—a great way to increase both their curiosity (WHY) and motivation to engage (WILL).

❓ What is the best way to address and manage classroom behaviors when children tend to feed off one another? How do I address students copying other students' inappropriate behavior?

While this is challenging, remember that one of the most valuable skills young children stand to learn is how to read and interact with others. Mastery of these WE Skills in the early childhood classroom commonly focuses on learning how to recognize and name other people's feelings. But WE Skill development can also, for better or for worse, involve copying other children's behaviors and testing to see what sort of responses various behaviors elicit.

In addition to putting WE to work, remember that it can take quite a bit of self-control (ME)—sometimes more than they typically have—for young children to be able to resist the impulse to copy what others are doing, even if they have been told to stop or when they know it's against the rules. For this, as well as just about any other disruptive or undesirable behavior, consider whether you might be able to turn it into a positive WE Skill opportunity by discussing with students how their behaviors might make you or their fellow students feel.

? What can I do when my students turn everything into a game and don't follow directions? How can we minimize distractions?

As we've discussed, one of the most common themes related to behavioral challenges has to do with rule-following, which primarily falls into the ME Skills category. When a child doesn't follow the rules, our response should always begin with considering where they are in their ME Skill development. How realistic is it to expect them to be able to control their impulses, refrain from a particular behavior or follow a certain set of instructions? The other thing to consider is not just how necessary any given rule is for what you ultimately want to achieve, but also at what cost when it comes to all of the other QI Skills. After all, too much focus on control runs the risk of limiting the development of pretty much all of the other QI Skills, from WHY, WILL and WIGGLE to WOBBLE and WHAT IF.

QI TAKEAWAYS:
CHALLENGING BEHAVIORS

- When approaching behavioral challenges, consider whether your expectations are aligned with what you know about children's QI Skill development.

- A significant number of challenging behaviors—from hitting, kicking, biting and throwing to interrupting, not sitting still and throwing tantrums—relate to young children's ME Skills (or the lack thereof).

- Creating an environment that supports QI Skill development means striking a balance between maintaining control and having children learn to follow the rules (ME Skills) and allowing them to actively interact, engage, explore, question, try new ways of doing things, and come up with new ideas (WE, WHY, WILL, WIGGLE, WOBBLE, WHAT IF).

QI REFLECTIONS:
CHALLENGING BEHAVIORS

- Think about the most challenging behaviors you've faced in your classroom. For each behavior, first consider whether correcting this behavior requires the ME ability to control one's thoughts, feelings or actions. How developmentally likely is it for the children in your classroom to be able to master the necessary ME Skills? How might you make it easier for them to master ME?

- For any behavior you consider to be challenging, try switching your perspective and see if you can identify any positive aspects of QI reflected in the behavior. For example, if a child isn't following instructions but happens to have come up with a really creative way of doing something, consider how you might address the negative behavior while at the same time not squelching their budding WHAT IF Skills.

- Think about your own QI Skills. Which ones do you rely on when dealing with challenging behaviors in your classroom? See if you can come up with ways you might better manage these behaviors by drawing on each of your own QI Skills.

WELCOMING QI SKILLS
INTO YOUR CLASSROOM

*"In learning you will teach, and
in teaching you will learn."*

PHIL COLLINS

TO BEGIN this last section, it seems only fitting to emphasize that QI Skills are not and were never meant to be something to consider or prioritize solely on "special" occasions. Their relevance extends well beyond those times when you find yourself facing challenging behaviors or when you are able to take a break from teaching to stop and think more deeply about your higher-level purpose, the universal right to play, or the meaning and importance of belongingness. All of those applications are important, of course, but first and foremost, QI Skills are meant to be fun. They're meant to be motivating, engaging, and easy to understand, so that you can apply them throughout the course of your day.

Seeing the QI in everyday classroom activities

Now that you have a good grasp on what the QI Skills actually are and why they are so valuable, one of the easiest things for you to do is to identify when, where and how they show up and how they could be enhanced as you make your way through each day in your classroom. We already did this with play: after going over some of the more definitional, academic and universal aspects of play, we discussed a new way of looking at play day-to-day in your classroom, one that allows you to see and appreciate all of the QI moments and opportunities that it offers.

Now, consider some of the additional activities and routines that define a typical day and which elements of QI might be involved. Here are a few examples to get you started:

Activities

- **Circle time.** Almost by definition, circle time requires young children to engage their ME Skills: they have to stop what they're doing, join the group, follow directions, pay attention, and resist the urge to interrupt and invade others' personal space. But the QI opportunities of circle time don't stop there. Think of all the social interaction and sharing of perspectives that bring WE front and center. Children are encouraged to ask questions to satisfy their curiosity (WHY) and fuel their motivation to learn (WILL). We can also use this time to allow them to apply other QI Skills like WIGGLE, by inviting children to physically interact with toys or other objects that correspond with the story or subject at hand.

- **Dress-up play.** All of the fanciful clothing and props involved makes this common form of play an inherently WIGGLE-enhancing one. As with just about any classroom activity involving more than one child, playing dress-up allows young children to practice both their ME and WE Skills. For example, children need to take turns, pay attention, and follow the "rules" of the dress-up game while listening to, communicating and sharing with others. And then there's all the pretending to be a teacher, a doctor, an astronaut or a parent, which offers all sorts of WHAT IF opportunities.

- **Story time.** At the risk of being repetitive, sitting and listening to a story while not poking or prodding one's friends clearly serves to exercise young children's budding ME Skills. Listening to stories about others—complete with descriptions of the characters' emotions, often enhanced by pictures that illustrate what each of those emotions looks like—makes reading aloud a particularly good way to help young children master the WE Skill of learning to read other people. You'll also be helping with the development of all their other QI Skills as well, such as WHY, by encouraging their curiosity and welcoming their questions; WIGGLE, by taking activities described in a book (such as gardening, baking, or puddle-jumping) and allowing children to partake in them in the real world; WOBBLE, as they see how characters in stories overcome obstacles and learn from their example; and WHAT IF, as, inspired by those same stories and your thought-provoking questions, they wonder about how their world could be different.

PLAY TAG WITH YOUR CURRICULUM

As a quick and easy extension of the QI strategies described above, consider taking a few extra minutes when reviewing your daily curriculum to tag it with each of the QI Skills. Are you finding a lot of ME and WE opportunities? That's common, but it's important to also identify and find opportunities to incorporate other QI Skills. This could be as simple as modeling WHY, making more time for WILL and WOBBLE, and encouraging WHAT IF. Make sure to find moments throughout the day to introduce, name, play with, encourage, and cultivate all of the QI Skills in your classroom.

Help children spread the word(s)

Now that you're well-equipped to make QI Skills an integral part of your classroom, I also want to emphasize the value in making sure that you're not only focused on simply assessing children's ability to demonstrate these skills for success, but on actually helping them understand and embrace them. In simple terms, that starts with teaching children about the QI Skills and having them join you as active participants in searching for, identifying and encouraging the QI Skills right alongside you.

I've seen this work impressively well in a school in Cornwall in the UK, where incoming four-year-olds are introduced to each of the QI Skills during their first week of class and within mere weeks are not only well-versed in what they are, but quite skilled at identifying them and even praising their classmates for their creative applications of each skill. At a community center in South Omaha, Nebraska, children and teachers alike enjoy taking their newly introduced QI Skills and creating a QI Skill wall. Under each QI Skill column on the wall, children and adults place sticky notes describing or depicting ways they have seen that skill come to life in their everyday experience at the center. In a Boston childcare center, motivated faculty didn't just settle for becoming well-versed in QI Skills and all the ways they could be brought into their classrooms and curriculum: they have taken to sending students home with "QI-grams," simple notes and observations celebrating students' daily QI Skills efforts, progress and accomplishments, to be shared with their parents.

QI TAKEAWAYS: EVERYDAY ACTIVITIES

- As soon as you start looking, you're likely to find QI Skills in just about every activity throughout the day.

- QI Skills are meant to be fun, engaging, motivating, and easy to understand and apply.

- Some QI Skills are more inherently present and easier to spot than others. ME, for example, factors heavily into most early childhood classroom routines; similarly, WE and the ability to "play well with others" are easily recognizable as defining features of preschool. Others, however, are more dependent on you making time for, facilitating, modeling, or creating the right conditions for them.

- Rather than committing to simply assessing children's QI Skills, be sure to focus your efforts on helping them understand, embrace and enjoy them.

QI REFLECTIONS: EVERYDAY ACTIVITIES

- Think about any aspect of your everyday classroom routine, from mealtime to reading aloud to planting a garden or free play on the playground. Consider how you would have described your chosen activity's purpose prior to learning about QI Skills. What would you have said children were getting out of it? Now, try to identify how various QI aspects might come into play with that same activity.

- How would you typically describe a successful day in your classroom? What would this look like for a student in your class? Do the criteria you use to define success more closely align with QI Skills, IQ Skills, or both?

It is my sincere hope that reading this book has given you even more reason to be proud of the ever-so-important job you do each and every day. I also hope that you feel more in control when it comes to focusing your day-to-day efforts on what really matters; that you have a clearer understanding of your students and are better able to enjoy the special relationship and interactions you have with them; and that you are all the more motivated to jump right in and start actively exploring new ways of engaging with your students around the QI Skills. You should feel encouraged and empowered to try out various approaches and activities to see which works best. This will allow you to be creative in how you bring QI Skills to life in your classroom, in the lives of your students, and in your own life as well.

May the force of the QI Skills be with you!

QI RESOURCES
AND REFERENCES

. . . .

I F YOUR WHY and WILL have you wanting to dive deeper, the following is a QI-Enhancing Strategies Quick Start Guide along with a sampling of books, organizations, and evidence-based resources that align well with the QI Skill concepts and framework you've been introduced to in this book.

QI-ENHANCING STRATEGIES QUICK START GUIDE

. . . .

T HE FOLLOWING LIST of overarching strategies applies
to all QI Skills. These strategies, along with those
specifically suggested in earlier chapters for each individual QI Skill, will allow you take advantage of all of the
everyday opportunities you have to nurture, encourage, and
develop QI Skills in your classroom.

Get to "it." Once you get into the swing of things, there's
practically an unlimited number of ways in which you can
bring each of the QI Skills into your daily classroom routines. When thinking about any given QI Skill (i.e., the "it"),
consider the many ways you (and your students) might better understand it, reflect on it, recognize it when you see it
in action, plan for it, praise it, practice it, prioritize it, model
it, sing it, read all about it, play with it, talk about it, repeat
it, share it ... you get the idea.

Apply a QI Skill lens. Challenge yourself to look at your
classroom, curriculum, routines, students, and even yourself through a QI Skill lens. You may find that you see all of
these things in a whole new, and hopefully more motivating,
empowering and engaging, light.

Come together around QI Skills. Remember, in the real world (which includes your classrooms) the QI Skills don't exist as clearly distinct entities or behaviors. Any given activity, whether that's reading aloud, gardening, an art project, a diaper change, or mealtime, is likely to offer a variety of QI Skill-enhancing opportunities. As soon as you start looking for them, you'll likely find that you're able to think about most any given activity and find ways to introduce, focus on and encourage several (if not all) of the QI Skills.

Look for hidden QI opportunities. Some QI Skills are fairly easy to identify and see playing out in your daily curriculum and classroom activities. Others, however, are more dependent on you facilitating, modeling, or creating the right conditions for them.

Model good QI behavior. Remember that "do as I say, not as I do" doesn't work well in just about any aspect of interacting with, guiding, or teaching young children (or adults, for that matter). This is definitely true when it comes to encouraging the use of QI Skills. If you don't make it a point to use, model, prioritize and embrace your own QI Skills, your students will inevitably be far less likely to develop theirs. Remember, their brains are wired to watch and learn, and you—as a caring, responsive adult—are key to the process of introducing new concepts and helping make the connections that will guide their development.

Consider parents (and other caregivers) to be QI allies. Creating an early childhood classroom environment in which young children are not just able but actively encouraged to try out, practice and develop their QI Skills is great. But what's even better is helping parents and other primary caregivers understand and support these same QI concepts and strategies. By sharing with them both why and how you are cultivating and bringing QI Skills to life in your classroom and with their children, you can help them see the value (and the fun) of doing so at home as well. Sharing your overall QI strategy with them can help prevent the perception that by spending time intentionally developing all of these essential but long undervalued skills, you are somehow not doing your job (which traditionally has been defined as just teaching the ABCs and 123s).

Reflect on your QI progress. Given that reflection has been recognized as a powerful tool for both professional and personal development, try to make it a daily habit to stop and reflect on the QI aspects of your day. Think about (better yet, write down and share) not just what you did to introduce and nurture QI Skills, but also how you and your students felt and reacted to your efforts. Consider what worked, what didn't, and why.

BOOKS

. . . .

Children's Books for Cultivating QI

As we've discussed, introducing young children to books is one of the very best ways to engage them with stories, emotions and experiences that will help them understand the world they live in and expand their worldview. Reading aloud with young children is about far more than just the book itself, the literal sounding out and sharing of words on a page, or helping them learn to read. It's also about cultivating a shared love of reading, and speaks to what we now know is at the very heart of nurturing the seven QI Skills that set children up for success: a shared, meaningful interaction that you can enjoy every day in your classroom.

If you have books tailored to the age and stage of development of children in your classroom, such as board books that babies and toddlers can touch, feel and drool on, then you're already off to a good start. Although there are countless wonderful children's books to choose from for any given classroom or age, certain books better illustrate QI Skills or encourage engaging them than others. As soon as you start looking, you'll also find that individual books often draw on multiple QI Skills, while WHY is a skill that is captured not just in the words of any given book, but also in children's inquisitiveness about, engagement with, and interest in *all* books.

The following list—which includes personal as well as friend- and colleague-recommended favorites alongside classic and contemporary books—is just a small sampling of what you can find when you start exploring the world of children's books with QI Skills in mind.

🖐 ❤ ? ♠ 𝒮 ◑ ✈
All of the QI Skills

Jumping Into Kindergarten by Julia Cook and Laura A. Jana, MD
If you're looking for a fun, lighthearted children's book dedicated solely to the introduction and practical application of all of the QI Skills, this is the one. I can say that with confidence, because I happened to write it specifically to serve as the first kid-friendly introduction of QI Skills. This is currently the only children's book available that does. (Stay tuned, as there may soon be more!) It's a school- and kindergarten-readiness book that follows a young kangaroo named Roo as he gets ready to jump into kindergarten, equipped with all of the really important (QI) skills in his invisible backpack. At the back of the book, you'll find a handy "Tips for Educators" summary of each of the QI Skills to have on hand as you read and discuss the book and all of the QI Skills with your students.

🖐 ME and ❤ WE

Baby Faces Board Book from DK Publishing
Both ME and WE Skills depend on the ability to recognize, understand and name emotions, which makes this "delightful book, full of fun faces just right for babies" an enjoyable (and durable) way to introduce very young children to such important emotions as happy, sad, puzzled, angry, worried, and several more.

Duck & Goose: Goose Needs a Hug by Tad Hills
In a literal sense, this simple tale is about a sad goose whose
feathered friends recognize that he's feeling sad, and try to
figure out just what it will take to make him happy again.
In a broad sense, it's about the relationships, ability to read
emotions, and ability to express empathy that are at the
heart of WE.

The Grouchy Ladybug by Eric Carle
Toddlers, teens and even adults feel grouchy sometimes.
Fortunately, those who share this story with young children
can help them not only recognize the emotion, but also learn
from the ill-tempered ladybug of the title the ME and WE
skills necessary to control socially unacceptable impulses,
just as the ladybug does. These include screaming, shouting,
refusing to share, and just generally not getting along.

I Say, You Say Feelings! by Tad Carpenter
This book focuses on the world of emotions: illustrations
and descriptions help children explore and hone their understanding of emotions.

It's Mine and **Little Blue and Little Yellow** by Leo Lionni
These two endearing books capture the power, importance
and challenge of learning WE Skills. The former focuses on
impulse control and learning to share, while the latter provides a colorful and simple (albeit somewhat abstract) view
of friendship, differences, and tolerance.

Teeth are Not for Biting; **Feet are Not for Kicking**;
Voices are Not for Yelling; and **Words are Not for Hurting**
by Elizabeth Verdick
A series of highly practical impulse- and self-control books.
Other good titles from Verdick include **Calm Down Time** and
Listening Time.

Hands are Not for Hitting by Martyn Agassi
This book dovetails nicely with Verdick's books above.

The ***When I Feel*** series by Cornelia Maude Spelman
These books address a range of emotions such as worried, angry, sad, scared, and jealous.

Sophie's Terrible Twos; ***Hands Off, Harry!***; and ***Yoko's World of Kindness*** by Rosemary Wells

All for Me and None for All; ***Me First***; and ***Listen, Buddy*** by Helen Lester

The Way I Feel by Janan Cain

The Way I Act by Steve Metzger

I Can Do It Too! by Karen Baicker

Go, Go, Go, Stop! by Charise Mericle Harper

A Color of His Own by Leo Lionni

Amazing Me: It's Busy Being Three!
by Julia Cook and Laura A. Jana

The Feelings Book by Todd Parr

Hurty Feelings by Helen Lester

My Many Colored Days by Dr. Seuss

How are You Peeling? Foods with Moods
by Saxton Freymann and Joost Elffers
This book offers a particularly appealing and unique way
to engage readers young and old alike, providing a literal
representation of various emotions while also serving as a
model of creativity by fruitfully putting produce to novel use.

When Sophie Gets Angry—Really, Really Angry and **When
Sophie's Feelings are Really, Really Hurt** by Molly Bang

Happy Hippo, Angry Duck: A Book of Moods
by Sandra Boynton

The Big Book of Hugs by Nick Ortner

A Great Big Cuddle by Michael Rosen
Poems for the very young.

My Heart is Like a Zoo by Michael Hall

Mine! by Sue Heap

Little Blue Truck by Alice Schertle

How Full is Your Bucket? For Kids by Tom Rath

Sign About baby sign language series by Anthony Lewis, which
includes **Getting Ready, Playtime, Meal Time** and **Going Out**

**Baby Signs: A Baby-Sized Introduction to Speaking With
Sign Language** illustrated by Joy Allen

〰 WIGGLE

What all the books below have in common is that they lend
themselves to being actively enjoyed in a very physical way.
They encourage children to clap, point to body parts, and
reach out to touch, feel, or jump along with the story. These
books foster children's early love of reading while also recognizing, in a very practical sense, that sometimes kids just
can't help but wiggle.

From Head to Toe by Eric Carle

Ten Tiny Toes by Caroline Jane Church

Pat-a-Cake and *We All Fall Down* by Mary Brigid Barrett

Jump, Frog, Jump! by Robert Kalan

Wheels on the Bus and *Shake My Sillies Out* by Raffi

Sign and Sing Along: Itsy-Bitsy Spider; *Head, Shoulders,
Knees and Toes*; *If You're Happy and You Know It*; and *This
Little Piggy* by Annie Kubler

Where is Baby's Belly Button? by Karen Katz

Baby Touch and Feel: Baby Animals from DK Publishing

The Itsy-Bitsy Spider by Rosemary Wells

DK Publishing Touch and Feel series, including *Colors and
Shapes, Animals, Baby Animals, Cuddly Animals, Bed-
time, Bathtime, Mealtime, Farm, Noisy Farm, First Words,
Numbers, Playtime, Splish! Splash!, Puppies and Kittens,
Trucks, Wild Animals* and *Things That Go*

❓ WHY, ⬆ WILL, ⬤ WOBBLE and 🚀 WHAT IF

Creatrilogy box set by Peter Reynolds
Right down to this trilogy's creative title, Reynolds makes it clear that he believes in the value of seeing the world differently, starting small, and the power of WHAT IF. *Ish* and *The Dot* have for years ranked high on my list of personal favorite books that illustrate how to cultivate children's creative spirit. *Sky Color*, the final book in the trilogy, encourages children to look beyond what's expected.

Oops! by Barney Saltzberg
What do you get from a book that proposes turning an accidental tear in a paper into the roaring mouth of an alligator, or taking a spill on a drawing and turning it into the shape of a goofy animal? The answer is a whimsically engaging book about WOBBLE meant to leave children and adult readers alike with the notion that "a mistake is an adventure in creativity" and "a portal of discovery."

The Little Engine That Could by Watty Piper
This classic children's book has WILL written all over it, from its very first "I think I can."

A Perfectly Messed Up Story by Patrick McDonnell
The use of both "perfectly" and "messed up" in the title should serve as a giveaway that this book—in characteristic McDonnell form—is about WOBBLE-ability and overcoming whatever obstacles we may meet (which in Little Louie's case comes in the form of a blob of jelly or chunky peanut butter) rather than pursuing perfection.

What Do You Do with an Idea? by Kobi Yamada
On the surface, this is a story of one brilliant idea and the child who helps to bring it into the world. However, in recognizing that children's ideas need nurturing just like children

do, Yamada starts in monotone but gradually introduces color and paints a picture of children's budding WHY and WHAT IF Skills and how they stand to change the world.

Beautiful Hands by Bret Baumgarten
Said to be inspired by the author's daily question to his young daughter, "What will your beautiful hands do today?" this inspiring book reinforces for children and adults the fundamental belief in a world full of endless possibilities and the power of WHAT IF.

Harold and the Purple Crayon by Crockett Johnson

Art by Patrick McDonnell

Perfect Square by Michael Hall

Horton Hatches the Egg by Dr. Seuss

The Most Magnificent Thing by Ashley Spires

Peep Leap by Elizabeth Verdick

The Artist Who Painted a Blue Horse by Eric Carle

QI books for grown-ups

Learning and Development
Heading Home with Your Newborn: From Birth to Reality
by Laura A. Jana and Jennifer Shu (American Academy of Pediatrics, 5th ed., 2025)
I co-authored this book with Jennifer Shu (who is also a pediatrician) to provide nuts-and-bolts insights and a reassuring support structure for practical, positive interactions and relationship-building with young children. Technically written for parents, the book is relevant and applicable for anyone who cares for infants.

How Children Succeed: Grit, Curiosity, and the Hidden Power of Character by Paul Tough

Mind in the Making: The Seven Essential Life Skills Every Child Needs by Ellen Galinsky

The Extended Mind: The Power of Thinking Outside the Brain by Annie Murphy Paul

The Philosophical Baby: What Children's Minds Tell Us About Truth, Love and the Meaning of Life by Alison Gopnik

The Play's the Thing: Teachers' Roles in Children's Play by Elizabeth Jones and Gretchen Reynolds, with series editor Sharon Ryan

The Science of Learning and Development: Enhancing the Lives of All Young People by Pamela Cantor and David Osher

The Whole Brain Child: 12 Revolutionary Strategies to Nurture Your Child's Developing Mind by Daniel J. Siegel, M.D. and Tina Payne Bryson

Other
Drive: The Surprising Truth About What Motivates Us by Daniel H. Pink

Mindset: The New Psychology of Success by Carol S. Dweck

ORGANIZATIONS

. . . .

American Academy of Pediatrics (AAP)

As a decades-long member and spokesperson for the AAP, I would be remiss if I didn't start this list by directing attention to the wealth of valuable and trustworthy sites and sources the AAP is dedicated to making available. These are not just for parents, but can be helpful for anyone invested in nurturing QI Skills as a key aspect of children's overall healthy growth and development. The AAP represents 67,000 pediatricians all committed to the optimal physical, mental, and social health and well-being of all infants and young children (as well as older children, adolescents, and even young adults). From early brain and child development and early-literacy-specific information to the AAP's extensive website, you can and should consider the AAP a go-to source for useful information.

www.healthychildren.org

Collaborative for Academic, Social, and Emotional Learning (CASEL)

Founded in 1994, CASEL is a non-profit, non-partisan organization with a long-standing commitment to establishing high-quality, evidence-based social and emotional learning (SEL) as an essential part of preschool through high school education.

www.casel.org

Center for Healthy Minds,
University of Wisconsin-Madison

Founded by neuroscientist Dr. Richard Davidson, the Center focuses on understanding the mind, emotions and well-being, and contributes to a growing body of research aimed at finding the best ways to support the well-being of young children and their caregivers. This includes exploring the importance of emotion regulation early in life for healthy social and decision-making skills throughout one's lifespan. Particularly relevant to some of the QI Skill concepts presented in this book, the Center is studying how mindfulness-based curricula (including the Center's own Kindness Curriculum) enhances young children's social and educational experiences:

www.centerhealthyminds.org

www.centerhealthyminds.org/science/studies/well-being-in-infants-and-children?archive=1

Centers for Disease Control & Prevention (CDC)

The CDC has long been considered the go-to source for information on the developmental milestones of early childhood, including those referenced in this book that are discussed in relation to QI Skills. Simply googling "Learn the Signs" will get you to the CDC's top-ranked webpage that lists the common motor, social-emotional, and cognitive milestones of early childhood broken down by age from two months to five years. You can also access printable milestone checklists translated into multiple languages and download a Milestone Tracker app.

www.cdc.gov/ncbddd/actearly/milestones

Center on the Developing Child, Harvard University
This is admittedly not somewhere to go for light bedtime or beach reading. But it is a definite go-to for anyone interested in and searching for supporting briefs, summaries of studies, and short videos that pull together essentially all that we know and that is being discovered about early brain and child development that offers such a strong foundation for the QI Skills framework.

www.developingchild.harvard.edu

- Executive Function: What Is Executive Function? And How Does it Relate to Child Development[149] (www.develop ingchild.harvard.edu/resources/infographics/what-is-executive-function-and-how-does-it-relate-to-child-development/)

- Building Adult Capacities to Enhance Child Outcomes (www.youtube.com/watch?v=urU-a_FsS5Y)

- The Brain's "Air Traffic Control" System: How Early Experiences Shape the Development of Executive Function (www.developingchild.harvard.edu/resources/working-paper/building-the-brains-air-traffic-control-system-how-early-experiences-shape-the-development-of-executive-function/)

- Brain Building Through Play: Activities for Infants, Toddlers and Children (www.developingchild.harvard.edu/resources/handouts-tools/brainbuildingthroughplay/)

National Association for the Education of Young Children (NAEYC)
As the leading professional membership organization for early childhood professionals, NAEYC is committed to promoting high-quality early learning for all young children by

connecting early childhood policy and research to everyday practice, as well as supporting early education professionals. The organization offers lots of useful books, online resources and learning opportunities, and hosts a large annual national conference.

www.naeyc.org

- Play Resources: www.naeyc.org/our-work/families/play

Reach Out and Read (ROR)

Reach Out and Read is a 501(c)3 non-profit that, for more than three decades, has been giving young children a foundation for success by incorporating books into pediatric care and encouraging families to read aloud together. As the only evidence-based national pediatric model focused on emotional connections endorsed by the American Academy of Pediatrics, Reach Out and Read serves children in all 50 states through 6,000 clinics and 33,000 clinicians.

ROR's decades of research confirms in no uncertain terms that positive interactions between caregivers and young children during shared reading experiences have proven to be effective in promoting children's early development, health and well-being. Among other things, be sure to check out on their "Resources for Families" page their offering of seasonal, age-divided booklists, each with tips for reading aloud.

www.reachoutandread.org

The Heckman Equation

The brainchild of Nobel Prize–winning University of Chicago economist James Heckman, this resource is equally great for early childhood educators who don't have an economics background. What Heckman and colleagues masterfully do, with support from the Pritzker Children's Initiative, is clearly and compellingly weave together the science showing why it is so critical for our children's (and our country's) future to invest in early childhood development. While the information it presents is likely not going to be of direct relevance in your day-to-day classroom endeavors, for anyone interested in exploring and understanding the economic case for investing in early childhood, Heckman's information is scientific, highly regarded, and also more easily accessible and understandable than what you might expect from a highly acclaimed economist.

www.heckmanequation.org

Tools of the Mind[150]
Founded over 30 years ago by developmental psychologists and based on a foundation of neuroscience meets (Vygotskian) developmental theory, Tools of the Mind offers actionable curriculum and teaching practices designed to enable children to learn how to learn while building the self-regulatory skills necessary for success in school and life.

www.toolsofthemind.org

Zero to Three
With a clearly defined age focus and expertise in translating the science of early childhood development into real impact, Zero to Three's mission is to ensure that all babies and toddlers have a strong start in life. Founded more than 45 years ago by leading researchers and clinicians, this is an organization you can turn to and trust. It boasts a very easy-to-navigate website that is full of practical, highly relevant, easy-to-read insights. Just head to the website and click on any of the organization's defined areas of focus, from child care, early development and well-being to the brain, early learning, equity and early intervention.

www.zerotothree.org

GLOSSARY

. . . .

Amygdala
The region of the brain primarily associated with emotional processes. Although the amygdala is best known for its involvement in fear and other emotions related to unpleasant stimuli, it is now known to be involved in positive emotions elicited by rewarding stimuli as well.[151]

CASEL
Founded in 1994, CASEL is a non-profit, non-partisan organization with a long-standing commitment to establishing high-quality, evidence-based social and emotional learning (SEL) as an essential part of preschool through high school education.[152]

CASEL 5 Framework
The CASEL 5 Framework is a set of five broad and interrelated areas of social-emotional competence that, according to CASEL, "can be taught and applied at various developmental stages from childhood to adulthood and across diverse cultural contexts." The framework includes self-awareness, self-management, social awareness, relationship skills, and responsible decision-making.[153]

Center for Healthy Minds

Founded and directed by world-renowned neuroscientist Dr. Ritchie Davidson, the Center for Healthy Minds at the University of Wisconsin-Madison was founded with the mission of cultivating well-being across the lifespan—from pregnancy to old age—through a scientific understanding of the mind. The Center's focus on well-being in infants and children involves the introduction of a new kind of ABCs based on *attention*, *breath*, and *calming*. The Center's research focuses on such topics as how early experiences influence the developing brain (Baby Brain and Behavior Project),[154] mindfulness training in children,[155] the impact of a kindness curriculum,[156] and understanding poverty's impact on the developing brain.[157]

Developmental milestones of early childhood

Skills such as taking a first step, smiling for the first time, and waving "bye bye" are called developmental milestones. Children reach these developmental milestones in how they play, learn, speak, act and move, and they're carefully tracked (or should be) by pediatricians, early educators and parents alike.

Emotional intelligence

The term "emotional intelligence" (EI) is broadly defined as the ability to perceive, use, understand, manage, and handle emotions. EI gained widespread popularity in the 1990s with the publication of the best-selling book *Emotional Intelligence* by psychologist and science journalist Daniel Goleman. It is typically broken down into four core components or abilities: self-awareness, self-management, social-awareness, and relationship management. Of note, Goleman not only recognized EI as representative of the skills and characteristics that drive leadership performance,[158] but he also went on to recognize EI's relevance to and importance in education, becoming one of the co-founders of CASEL.

Emotional literacy

Recognized as a vital skill on par with traditional literacy, emotional literacy is the ability to understand, express, and regulate emotion. The term is sometimes used interchangeably with "emotional intelligence."

Executive function skills

A group of complex mental processes and cognitive abilities defined by working memory, impulse inhibition, and cognitive flexibility. These are the skills required for reasoning and goal-directed behavior. As summarized by Harvard's Center on the Developing Child, "These skills underlie the capacity to plan ahead and meet goals, display self-control, follow multiple-step directions even when interrupted, and stay focused despite distractions, among others."

Extrinsic motivation

This describes a motivation that's based on meeting an external goal, garnering praise and approval, winning a competition, or receiving an award or payment.[159] With extrinsic motivation, completion of a task or behavior is driven either by the promise of a reward (which can be tangible, such as money, or intangible, such as praise), or fueled by the desire to avoid a negative outcome, consequence, or punishment.[160]

Failure resume

Sometimes referred to as an "anti-portfolio" or "CV of failures," a failure resume is an increasingly popular way of formally accounting for one's past mistakes and failures for the purpose of learning from them. Failure resumes are based on the belief that thinking about how and why things went awry helps us better learn from, innovate and imagine alternative circumstances.

Fixed mindset

The belief, identified by researcher and *Mindset* author Carol Dweck, that your basic qualities are things you are born with and have no control over (hence fixed), rather than things you can cultivate through your efforts (growth).

Foundational skills

Foundational learning skills refer to the skills that make learning possible. Foundational skills standards have traditionally included print concepts, phonological awareness, phonics and word recognition, and fluency.[161]

Growth mindset

The belief, introduced by researcher and *Mindset* author Carol Dweck, that your basic qualities are things you can cultivate through dedication and hard work (hence growth), rather than things you are born with and have no control over (fixed).

Intrinsic motivation

Being motivated to engage in an activity for its own sake.[162] The researchers credited with developing the concept of intrinsic motivation defined it as "the doing of an activity for its inherent satisfaction rather than for some separable consequence. When intrinsically motivated, a person is moved to act for the fun or challenge rather than because of external products, pressures, or rewards." This concept, developed as part of Self Determination Theory, served to overturn the prevailing (behaviorist) belief that people performed their best when given external rewards, finding instead that one's own thoughts and feelings are far more motivating.[163]

IQ Skills
IQ Skills refer to all of the traditionally recognized reading-, writing-, and arithmetic-type skills that rely on more concrete, fact-based content and technical knowledge. As a concept I introduced (at the same time as QI Skills) as a way to more concisely describe all of these commonly recognized "academic" skills, IQ Skills are in no way formally related to Intelligence Quotients, traditional "IQ" scores, or the formal standardized testing designed to assess human intelligence. Rather, they represent skills that are complementary to the QI Skills.

Joint attention
Also called "shared attention," joint attention involves two people purposefully focusing their attention on the same thing, such as an object or person, as part of a shared social interaction. This ability to focus, shift and maintain one's attention as a shared activity with someone else starts to develop soon after birth. It represents an important form of early social and communicative behavior, and serves to facilitate the development of cognitive and other valuable skills, such as bonding and perspective-taking.

Knowledge-based economy
A knowledge-based economy is one in which knowledge is produced, disseminated, and used, and a key factor in growth, wealth creation, and employment; and where human capital is the driver of creativity, innovation, and the generation of new ideas, with information and communication technology (ICT) serving as an enabler.[164]

Mischel's Marshmallow Test

Landmark research begun in the 1960s by Stanford psychologist Walter Mischel designed to test and ultimately better understand the development of self-control and deferred gratification in preschoolers, and whether children's early abilities to resist the temptation of a marshmallow (and for how long) had implications for their future life outcomes.

Mirror neurons

These specialized brain cells are activated when someone participates in physical (motor) activity and also when we observe others performing the same or a similar motor activity. First discovered in monkeys, subsequent studies in human infants suggest that the mirror neuron system develops in the first year, and that it plays an important role in helping infants and adults alike understand other people's actions. For this reason, mirror neurons are considered by some as one of this century's most important neuroscientific discoveries.[165]

Prefrontal cortex

Recognized as the most evolved part of the human brain and home to the executive function skills, the prefrontal cortex (PFC) is responsible for regulating thoughts, actions, and emotions. Among its many functions, it serves as a "mental sketch pad," making it possible to not only retain or bring to mind recent or past events, but also to use this knowledge to regulate behaviors, thoughts and emotions accordingly.[166]

"Serve-and-return"

Commonly used in the context of early brain and child development, this term describes responsive, back-and-forth interactions between children and their caregivers that shape brain architecture.[167]

Social-emotional learning (SEL)
Social and emotional learning is "the process through which all young people and adults acquire and apply the knowledge, skills, and attitudes to develop healthy identities, manage emotions and achieve personal and collective goals, feel and show empathy for others, establish and maintain supportive relationships, and make responsible and caring decisions." Recognized as an integral part of both human development and education, SEL is commonly defined by its five core components (the "CASEL 5"; see above): (1) self-awareness, (2) self-management, (3) social awareness, (4) relationship skills, and (5) responsible decision-making.[168]

Spaghetti Marshmallow Challenge
A simple, 18-minute team-building activity that involves using dry spaghetti and a single large marshmallow to construct a tower. The exercise is designed to encourage creative and collective problem-solving while illustrating the value of agility, hands-on learning, and resilience.

Synapse
Technically defined as the point at which electrical signals move from one nerve cell to another,[169] synapses are where neurons connect and communicate with each other. Each neuron has anywhere between a few to hundreds of thousands of connections with themselves, neighboring neurons, or neurons in other regions of the brain.[170]

ABOUT THE AUTHOR

D R. LAURA A. JANA is an internationally renowned U.S.-based pediatrician, early childhood expert, and award-winning author of more than 30 books for parents, educators, and children. She first gained international recognition working alongside the iconic Dr. Benjamin Spock and has spent the past 25+ years translating the science of early development into real-world strategies for raising and educating thriving children.

Dr. Jana most recently served as Chief Innovation Officer at Penn State University's Evidence to Impact Collaborative, and has advised national childcare companies, global toy brands, and nonprofit and government organizations dedicated to improving the lives of children and families. A longtime early literacy advocate and former nine-year owner of a 200-student educational childcare center, she also serves as a media spokesperson for the American Academy of Pediatrics and is a trusted consultant across academia, policy, and industry.

Dr. Jana's most recent books—including *QI Skills for the Early Childhood Classroom*, *The Toddler Brain*, and *Jumping Into Kindergarten*—focus on nurturing the foundational human skills children need to thrive in a rapidly changing, AI-powered world. She has delivered over 100 talks and keynotes across five continents, including presentations at the World Forum on Early Childhood, the U.S. Chamber of Commerce, the World Bank, Early Childhood Australia, the Delhi Public Schools, the NASDAQ Entrepreneurial Center, and the British Parliament.

QI NOTES

· · · · · · · · · · · · ·

1   C.A. Nelson, 2000. "In Brief: The Science of Early Childhood Development." Accessed from Harvard University's Center on the Developing Child. https://developingchild.harvard.edu/resources/inbrief-science-of-ecd/.

2   Adele Diamond, W. Steven Barnett, Jessica Thomas and Sarah Munro, "Preschool Program Improves Cognitive Control," *Science* 318, no. 5855 (November 30, 2007): 1387-1388.

3   Institute for Social Capital, "Shared Language," *Social Capital Research.* Accessed August 24, 2024. https://www.socialcapitalresearch.com/explore-social-capital/predispositions/shared-language/#:~:text=Shared%20language%20serves%20as%20the,aimed%20at%20achieving%20shared%20goals.

4   Committee on the Science of Children Birth to Age 8: Deepening and Broadening the Foundation for Success, Board on Children, Youth, and Families, Institute of Medicine, and National Research Council, *Transforming the Workforce for Children Birth Through Age 8: A Unifying Foundation.* Edited by L.R. Allen and B.B. Kelly (Washington, DC: National Academies Press, 2015). https://www.ncbi.nlm.nih.gov/books/NBK310550/.

5   "Qi." Wikipedia. Last modified August 21, 2024. https://en.wikipedia.org/wiki/Qi.

6   Collaborative for Academic, Social, and Emotional Learning (CASEL), "Fundamentals of SEL." Accessed August 24, 2024. https://casel.org/fundamentals-of-sel/

7   Harvard University Center on the Developing Child, "What Is Executive Function and How Does It Relate to Child Development?" Accessed August 28, 2024. https://developingchild.harvard.edu/resources/what-is-executive-function-and-how-does-it-relate-to-child-development/.

8   Harvard University Center on the Developing Child, "What Is Executive Function and How Does It Relate to Child Development?" Accessed

August 28, 2024. https://developingchild.harvard.edu/resources/what-is-executive-function-and-how-does-it-relate-to-child-development/.

9   Bruce Wexler, *Brain and Culture: Neurobiology, Ideology, and Social Change* (Cambridge, MA: MIT Press, 2006).

10 Drake Bennett, "What Does the Marshmallow Test Actually Test?" *Bloomberg News*, October 17, 2012. Accessed August 24, 2024. https://www.bloomberg.com/news/articles/2012-10-17/what-does-the-marshmallow-test-actually-test?embedded-check-out=true. (Subscription required.)

11 B.J. Casey, L.H. Somerville, I.H. Gotlib, O. Ayduk, N.T. Franklin, M.K. Askren, J. Jonides et al, "Behavioral and Neural Correlates of Delay of Gratification 40 Years Later," *Proceedings of the National Academy of Sciences* 108, no. 36 (July 2011): 14998-15003. https://doi.org/10.1073/pnas.1108561108.

12 History.com Editors, "*Sesame Street* Debuts," *History*. 1969. Accessed August 24, 2024. https://www.history.com/this-day-in-history/sesame-street-debuts.

13 Rosemarie Truglio, PhD, phone conversation with the author, May 16, 2016.

14 "Get Lost, Mr. Chips." *Sesame Street*, Season 43, episode 4301. Aired September 24, 2012, on PBS. Accessed August 24, 2024. https://www.sesamestreetguide.com/2020/07/sesame-street-episode-4301.html.

15 Sam Stein, "The Scientist Who Taught Cookie Monster Self Control Has a Warning for Congress," *HuffPost*, September 18, 2015. https://www.huffpost.com/entry/marshmallow-test-science-funding_n_55fc2a1ee4b00310edf6b4d3.

16 Deborah L. Linebarger and Rachael Gatewood, *Lessons from Cookie Monster: Educational Television, Executive Function, and Preschoolers* (Iowa City, IA: University of Iowa, 2014).

17 *Sesame Street*, "Me Want It (But Me Wait)." YouTube video, 3:10. August 5, 2013. https://youtu.be/9PnbKL3wuH4.

18 Terrie E. Moffit, Louise Arseneault, Daniel Belsky, Nigel Dickson, Robert J. Hancox, HonaLee Harrington, Renate Houts et al, "A Gradient of Childhood Self-Control Predicts Health, Wealth, and Public Safety," *Proceedings of the National Academy of Sciences* 108, no. 7 (February 15, 2011): 2693-98.

19 Angela Lee Duckworth, "Grit: The Power of Passion and Perseverance." TED Talk, April 2013, 6:12. https://www.ted.com/talks/angela_lee_duckworth_the_key_to_success_grit?language.com+env.

20 T. W. Watts, Gregory J. Duncan and H. Quan, "Revisiting the Marshmallow Test: A Conceptual Replication Investigating Links Between Early Delay of Gratification and Later Outcomes," *Psychological Science* 29, no. 7 (July 2018): 1159-1177. https://doi.

org/10.1177/0956797618761661. Epub May 25, 2018. PMID: 29799765; PMCID: PMC6050075.

21 University of California–Santa Barbara, "Happiness Challenge: Mindfulness." Accessed August 28, 2024. https://wellness.ucsb.edu/challenges/happiness-challenge/ucsb-happiness-challenge/happiness-challenge-mindfulness.

22 L. Flook, S. B. Goldberg, L. Pinger and R. J. Davidson, "Promoting Prosocial Behavior and Self-Regulatory Skills in Preschool Children through a Mindfulness-Based Kindness Curriculum," *Developmental Psychology* 51, no. 1 (January 2015): 44-51. https://doi.org/10.1037/a0038256.

23 Bill Duane, quoted in Laszlo Bock, *Work Rules!: Insights from Inside Google That Will Transform How You Live and Lead* (New York: Hachette Book Group, 2015).

24 Y. Chen and Linda Smith. "The Social Origins of Sustained Attention in One-Year-Old Human Infants," *Current Biology* 26, no. 9 (May 9, 2016): 1235-1240. https://doi.org/10.1016/j.cub.2016.03.007.

25 Elizabeth Jones and Gretchen Reynolds, *The Play's the Thing: Teachers' Roles in Children's Play* (Early Childhood Education Series), 2nd ed. (New York: Teachers College Press, 2011), 36.

26 Kelly April Tyrell, "Kindness Curriculum Boosts School Success in Preschoolers," School of Education, University of Wisconsin-Madison, February 3, 2015. https://www.education.wisc.edu/soe/research/research-news/2015/02/03/kindness-curriculum-boosts-school-success-in-preschoolers.

27 Adele Diamond and Daphne S. Ling, "Conclusions about Interventions, Programs, and Approaches for Improving Executive Functions That Appear Justified and Those That, Despite Much Hype, Do Not," *Developmental Cognitive Neuroscience* 18 (2016): 34-48. https://doi.org/10.1016/j.dcn.2016.02.002.

28 Patricia A. Jennings et al, "Impacts of the CARE for Teachers Program on Teachers' Social and Emotional Competence and Classroom Interactions," *Journal of Educational Psychology* 109, no. 7 (2017): 1010-28. As cited in Maria Gehl and Aidan H. Bohlander, "Rocking and Rolling. Being Present: Mindfulness in Infant and Toddler Settings," *Young Children* 73, no. 1 (March 2018). Accessed August 26, 2024. https://www.naeyc.org/resources/pubs/yc/mar2018/rocking-and-rolling#:~:text=Deep%20belly%20breathing%3A%20put%20your,the%20muscles%20in%20your%20body.

29 Jon Kabat-Zinn, *Wherever You Go, There You Are: Mindfulness Meditation in Everyday Life* (New York: Hyperion, 1994), as cited in Gehl and Bohlander, "Rocking and Rolling. Being Present: Mindfulness in Infant and Toddler Settings." *Young Children* 73, no. 1 (March 2018). Accessed August 26, 2024. https://www.naeyc.org/resources/pubs/yc/mar2018/

rocking-and-rolling#:~:text=Deep%20belly%20breathing%3A%20put%20 your,the%20muscles%20in%20your%20body.

30 Daniel J. Siegel, "Relationship, Science, and Being Human," Dr. Dan Siegel (blog). Accessed August 26, 2024. https://drdansiegel.com/ relationship-science-and-being-human/.

31 Julian Treasure, "Five Ways to Listen Better." TED Talk, July 2011, 7:50. https://www.ted.com/talks/ julian_treasure_5_ways_to_listen_better.

32 N. Duchesneau, *Social, Emotional, and Academic Development through an Equity Lens* (Washington, DC: Education Trust, 2020), as cited in K. M. Gagnier, Al Okawa and S. Jones-Manson, *Designing and Implementing Social Emotional Learning Programs to Promote Equity* (White paper produced by Anwar and the Office of Elementary and Secondary Education; Education, Innovation, and Research Program [EIR], 2022).

33 Paul H. Lipkin et al, "Evidence-Informed Milestones for Developmental Surveillance Tools," *Pediatrics* 149, no. 3 (March 2022): e2021052138, https://doi.org/10.1542/peds.2021-052138.

34 Centers for Disease Control and Prevention (CDC), "Milestones," *Learn the Signs. Act Early.*, National Center on Birth Defects and Developmental Disabilities. Last reviewed February 17, 2023. https://www.cdc.gov/ ncbddd/actearly/milestones/index.html.

35 Jones et al, 2017, and Ramirez et al, 2021, as cited in Gagnier, Okawa and Jones-Manson, *Designing and Implementing Social Emotional Learning Programs.*

36 D. E. Jones, Mark Greenberg and M. Crowley, "Early Social-Emotional Functioning and Public Health: The Relationship between Kindergarten Social Competence and Future Wellness," *American Journal of Public Health* 105, no. 11 (November 2015): 2283–90.

37 Jones, Greenberg and Crowley, "Early Social-Emotional Functioning," 2283–90.

38 Reid Hoffman and Ben Casnocha, *The Start-Up of You: Adapt to the Future, Invest in Yourself, and Transform Your Career* (New York: Crown Business, 2012), 87–88.

39 Pat Levitt, PhD, presentation at the U.S. Chamber of Commerce, June 21, 2017 (attended by author).

40 Rechele Brooks and Andrew N. Meltzoff, "The Development of Gaze Following and Its Relation to Language," *Developmental Science* 8, no. 6 (2005): 535–43.

41 Allison Gabbier and Heather Bortfeld, "Revisiting How We Operationalize Joint Attention," *Infant Behavior and Development* 63 (May 2021): 101566, https://doi.org/10.1016/j.infbeh.2021.101566. Published by Elsevier.

42 Alison Gopnik, "Empathic Civilization: Amazing Empathic Babies," The Blog (blog), *Huffington Post*, April 26, 2010. http://www.huffingtonpost. com/alison-gopnik/empathic-civilization-ama_b_473961.html.

43 Tools of the Mind. Accessed August 28, 2024. https://www.toolsofthe-mind.org.

44 Mary Helen Immordino-Yang, *Emotions, Learning, and the Brain: Exploring the Educational Implications of Affective Neuroscience* (The Norton Series on the Social Neuroscience of Education) (New York: W.W. Norton & Company, 2011).

45 "Empathy Documentary – Barack Obama Promotes Empathy from Books and Literacy." YouTube video, 2:03. Posted by Edwin Rutsch, August 27, 2010. https://www.youtube.com/watch?v=tg_qt_ P8B40&list=PL1D8ZVLata8h3YDa-0A4B9ha4Vl6kNB_W&index=4.

46 Larry Ferlazzo, "'A More Beautiful Question': An Interview With Warren Berger," *Education Week*, July 16, 2014. https://www.edweek.org/ teaching-learning/opinion-a-more-beautiful-question-an-interview-with-warren-berger/2014/07.

47 Olivier Serrat, *The Five Whys Technique* (Manila, Philippines: Asian Development Bank, February 2009). http://www.adb.org/sites/default/ files/publication/27641/five-whys-technique.pdf .

48 Serrat, *The Five Whys Technique*.

49 Clayton Christensen, Jeff Dyer and Hal Gregersen, *The Innovator's DNA: Mastering the Five Skills of Disruptive Innovators* (Boston: Harvard Business Review Press, 2011), 77.

50 Warren Berger, "Why Curious People Are Destined for the C-Suite," *Harvard Business Review*, September 11, 2015. https://hbr. org/2015/09/why-curious-people-are-destined-for-the-c-suite

51 Jeffrey H. Dyer, Hal Gregersen and Clayton M. Christensen, "The Innovator's DNA," *Harvard Business Review*, December 2009. https://hbr. org/2009/12/the-innovators-dna.

52 Christensen, Dyer and Gregersen, *The Innovator's DNA*, 71.

53 Ferlazzo, "'A More Beautiful Question': An Interview With Warren Berger."

54 Paul Harris, "What Children Learn from Questioning," *Educational Leadership* 73, no. 1 (September 2015): 24-29. https://ascd.org/el/articles/ what-children-learn-from-questioning.

55 https://www.library.hbs.edu/hc/polaroid/instant-photography/ the-idea-of-instant-photography/

56 Harvard Business School Baker Library, "The Idea of Instant Photography," *Polaroid Project: Harvard Business School*. Accessed August 28, 2024. https://www.library.hbs.edu/hc/polaroid/instant-photography/ the-idea-of-instant-photography/.

57 Fred Rogers, quoted in Gregg Behr and Ryan Rydzewski, *When You Wonder, You're Learning: Mister Rogers' Enduring Lessons for Raising Creative, Curious, Caring Kids* (New York: Hachette Go, 2021).
58 Behr and Rydzewski, *When You Wonder, You're Learning*, 23.
59 Christensen, Dyer and Gregersen, *The Innovator's DNA*, 74.
60 J.K. Rowling, 2008 Harvard commencement speech, quoted in Tom Popomaronis, "Harry Potter Novelist J.K. Rowling's Famous Advice to Harvard Students Is Dark but So Brilliant and True," CNBC, March 28, 2019, https://www.cnbc.com/2019/03/28/harry-potter-novelist-jk-rowling-famous-advice-to-harvard-students-is-dark-but-so-brilliant-and-true.html.
61 Daniel H. Pink, *Drive: The Surprising Truth About What Motivates Us* (New York: Riverhead Books, 2011).
62 Homer Rice, quoted in Pink, *Drive*.
63 Pink, *Drive*.
64 Pink, *Drive*.
65 Watty Piper, *The Little Engine That Could* (New York: Philomel Books, 2005).
66 Dave Coverly, "Speed Bump." Cartoon, image no. 116565, September 25, 2014.
67 Nilofer Merchant, "Got a Meeting? Take a Walk." TED Talk, February 2013, 3:27. https://www.ted.com/talks/nilofer_merchant_got_a_meeting_take_a_walk.
68 Nilofer Merchant, "Sitting Is the Smoking of Our Generation," *Harvard Business Review*, January 14, 2013, https://hbr.org/2013/01/sitting-is-the-smoking-of-our-generation.
69 Paul, *The Extended Mind*, 47.
70 Paul, *The Extended Mind*, 47.
71 Henry David Thoreau, *Thoreau: A Book of Quotations* (Mineola, NY: Dover Publications, 2001).
72 M. Oppezzo and D.L. Schwartz, "Give Your Ideas Some Legs: The Positive Effect of Walking on Creative Thinking," *Journal of Experimental Psychology: Learning, Memory and Cognition* 40, no. 4 (2014): 1142-1152. http://www.apa.org/pubs/journals/releases/xlm-a0036577.pdf.
73 R. Tanaka and S. Noi, "Effects of Using Standing Desks for 45 Minutes on the Stress and Executive Function of Elementary School Students," *PLOS ONE* 17, no. 8 (2022): e0272035. https://doi.org/10.1371/journal.pone.0272035.
74 L. Bolz, S. Heigele and J. Bischofberger, "Running Improves Pattern Separation during Novel Object Recognition," *Brain Plasticity* 1, no. 1 (2015): 129-141.

75 E.M. Hunter and C. Wu, "Give Me a Better Break: Choosing Workday Break Activities to Maximize Resource Recovery," *Journal of Applied Psychology* 10, no. 2 (2016): 302-311. https://doi.org/10.1037/ap10000045.

76 Christensen, Dyer and Gregersen, *The Innovator's DNA*.

77 Pooja S. Tandon, Brian E. Saelens and Dimitri A. Christakis, "Active Play Opportunities at Child Care," *Pediatrics* (May 2015). https://doi.org/10.1542/peds.2014-2750.

78 University of Florida College of Education, *History of Children's Board Books*. Accessed August 27, 2024. https://social.shorthand.com/UF_COE/n2eopZzdjn/history-of-childrens-board-books.html#:~:text=.

79 J.J. Meade, "The History of the Bendable, Durable, Chewable Board Book," *Literary Hub*, August 26, 2021. https://lithub.com/the-history-of-the-bendable-durable-chewable-board-book/.

80 Rachel Y. Moon, MD, FAAP, "How to Keep Your Sleeping Baby Safe: AAP Policy Explained," *American Academy of Pediatrics*. Last updated October 25, 2023. https://www.healthychildren.org/English/ages-stages/baby/sleep/Pages/a-parents-guide-to-safe-sleep.aspx#:~:-text=Swaddle%20your%20baby%20if%20you,breathe%20or%20move%20their%20hips.

81 Administration for Children & Families Office of Child Care, *CCDF Health and Safety Requirements Fact Sheet: Reducing the Risk of Sudden Infant Death Syndrome and Using Safe Sleeping Practices*, U.S. Department of Health & Human Services. Accessed August 27, 2024, https://childcareta.acf.hhs.gov/sites/default/files/259_1508_healthsafety_summary_sids_final.pdf.

82 Arthur M. Glenberg, "How Reading Comprehension Is Embodied and Why That Matters," *International Electronic Journal of Elementary Education* 4, no. 1 (2011): 5-18. Accessed August 27, 2024. https://files.eric.ed.gov/fulltext/EJ1070457.pdf.

83 Art Glenberg, PhD, *ASU Department of Psychology – Laboratory for Embodied Cognition*, Arizona State University. https://psychology.asu.edu/research/labs/embodied-cognition-lab-glenberg .

84 Kathy Hirsh-Pasek, Department of Psychology and Human Development, Temple University, is credited with coining the phrase "hands on, minds on," which highlights the importance of active, engaged learning.

85 "*Time*'s 100 Greatest Toys of All Time," *Time*. Accessed August 27, 2024.https://content.time.com/time/specials/packages/completelist/0,29569,2049243,00.html.

86 "Weeble." Wikipedia. Last modified August 26, 2024. https://en.wikipedia.org/wiki/Weeble.

87 Kathy Chin Leong, "Google Reveals Its 9 Principles of Innovation," *Fast Company*, November 20, 2013. http://www.fastcompany.com/3021956/how-to-be-a-success-at-everything/googles-nine-principles-

of-innovation.

88 Smith College, "Failing Well: Campus Series Helps Students Rethink Setbacks," *Smith College News.* Accessed August 27, 2024. https://www .smith.edu/news-events/news/ failing-well-campus-series-helps-students-rethink-setbacks.

89 J.V. Matso, "Failure 101: Rewarding Failure in the Classroom to Stimulate Creative Behavior," *Journal of Creative Behavior* 25, no. 1 (March 1991): 82-85.

90 Wendy Mogel, *The Blessing of a Skinned Knee* (New York: Penguin Group, 1988).

91 Tom Wujec, *Marshmallow Challenge.* Accessed August 27, 2024. https:// www.tomwujec.com/marshmallow-challenge.

92 Tom Wujec, "Build a Tower, Build a Team." TED Talk, March 2010, 6:34. https://www.ted.com/talks/ tom_wujec_build_a_tower_build_a_team?subtitle=en.

93 Ken Robinson, "Do Schools Kill Creativity?" TED Talk, February 2006, 19:11. Accessed August 28, 2024, https://www.ted.com/talks/ ken_robinson_says_schools_kill_creativity?language=en.

94 American Psychological Association, "Creativity." Adapted from *APA Dictionary of Psychology.* Accessed August 27, 2024. https://www.apa.org/ topics/creativity#:~:text=Creativity%20is%20the%20ability%20to,or%20 solution%20to%20a%20problem.

95 Jean Piaget, "Biological Evolution and Cognitive Development." Speech presented at the International Conference on Cognitive Development, Kyoto, Japan, 1971.

96 Sir Ken Robinson, "All Our Futures: Creativity, Culture and Education." Presentation at the 2015 World Creativity Forum, Thelma Gaylord Performing Arts Theater, Oklahoma City, OK, March 31, 2015.

97 Hoffman and Casnocha, *The Start-up of You,* 3.

98 Michael Platt, *The Leader's Brain* (New York: HarperCollins, 2014), chap 4: "Harnessing the Brain's 'Innovation Engine'."

99 John S. Hutton, Tzipi Horowitz-Kraus, Alan L. Mendelsohn, To DeWitt, Scott K. Holland and the C-MIND Authorship Consortium, "Home Reading Environment and Brain Activation in Preschool Children Listening to Stories," *Pediatrics* 126, no. 3 (September 2015): 466-478.

100 Peter Diamandis, "Raising Kids During Exponential Times," *Peter Diamandis Blog,* January 28, 2015. https://peterdiamandis.tumblr.com/ post/124671688543/raising-kids-during-exponential-times.

101 "Creativity." *Stanford Encyclopedia of Philosophy.* Published February 16, 2023. https://plato.stanford.edu/entries/creativity/.

102 World Economic Forum, *Future of Jobs Report 2023* (Geneva: World Economic Forum, 2023). https://www3.weforum.org/docs/WEF_ Future_of_Jobs_2023.pdf.

103 IBM, "2010 Global CEO Study: Creativity Selected as Most Crucial Factor for Future Success," *PR Newswire,* September 21, 2010.https://

www.prnewswire.com/news-releases/ibm-2010-global-ceo-study-
creativity-selected-as-most-crucial-factor-for-future-success-
94028284.html.

104 Berger, "Why Curious People Are Destined for the C-Suite."

105 Richard Florida, *The Rise of the Creative Class: And How It's Transforming
Work, Leisure, Community, and Everyday Life* (New York: Basic Books,
2002).

106 Virginia Heffernan, "Education Needs a Digital Age
Upgrade," *The New York Times*, August 7, 2011. https://archive.
nytimes.com/opinionator.blogs.nytimes.com/2011/08/07/
education-needs-a-digital-age-upgrade/?partner=rss&emc=rss.

107 Robinson, "Do Schools Kill Creativity?"

108 Michele Root-Bernstein, "Imaginary Worldplay as an Indicator of
Creative Giftedness," in *International Handbook on Giftedness*, ed. Larisa
V. Shavinina (Dordrecht, Netherlands: Springer Netherlands, 2009),
599-616.

109 A.V. Sosa, "Association of the Type of Toy Used during Play with
the Quantity and Quality of Parent-Infant Communication," *JAMA
Pediatrics*. Published online December 23, 2015. https://doi.org/10.1001/
jamapediatrics.2015.3753.

110 "Creativity." *Cambridge Dictionary*. Accessed August 27, 2024. https://
dictionary.cambridge.org/us/dictionary/english/creativity.

111 Adele Diamond, quoted in Ellen Galinsky, *Mind in the Making: The Seven
Essential Life Skills Every Child Needs* (New York: HarperCollins, 2010), 9.

112 Krista Tippett, host, interview with Rex Jung, "Creativity and
the Everyday Brain," *On Being*, audio blog, March 22, 2012.
Transcript posted August 20, 2015. https://onbeing.org/programs/
rex-jung-creativity-and-the-everyday-brain/.

113 Office of the United Nations High Commissioner for Human Rights,
Convention on the Rights of the Child. General Assembly Resolution 44/25
of November 20, 1989. Accessed August 27, 2024. https://www.ohchr.
org/en/instruments-mechanisms/instruments/convention-rights-child.

114 Office of the United Nations High Commissioner for Human Rights,
Convention on the Rights of the Child, Article 31.

115 United Nations, "Children." Accessed August 27, 2024. https://www.
un.org/en/global-issues/children.

116 Oxford Learner's Dictionaries, "Play." Accessed August 27, 2024. https://
www.oxfordlearnersdictionaries.com/definition/english/play_1.

117 Oxford Learner's Dictionaries, "Play." Accessed August 27, 2024. https://
www.oxfordlearnersdictionaries.com/definition/english/play_1.

118 Merriam-Webster, "Play." Accessed August 27, 2024. https://www.merri-
am-webster.com/dictionary/play.

119 Human Kinetics, "Definitions of Leisure, Play, and Recreation." Accessed

August 27, 2024. https://us.humankinetics.com/blogs/excerpt/
definitions-of-leisure-play-and-recreation.

120 Peter Gray, "Definitions of Play," *Scholarpedia* 8, no. 7 (2013):
30578. https://doi.org/10.4249/scholarpedia.30578.

121 B. Sparrow, "What Really Matters: The Teacher in the Concentrated
Encounter," in *Reading, Writing, and Talking with Four, Five, and Six Year
Olds,* ed. Elizabeth Jones (Pasadena, CA: Pacific Oaks College, 1988),
234. Quoted in Jones and Reynolds, *The Play's the Thing*, 48.

122 Early Childhood Australia, *ECA Statement on Play.* Accessed August
28, 2024. https://www.earlychildhoodaustralia.org.au/our-work/
eca-statement-on-play/.

123 Kenneth R. Ginsburg, MD, MSEd, and the Committee on
Communications and the Committee on Psychosocial Aspects of
Child and Family Health of the American Academy of Pediatrics, "The
Importance of Play in Promoting Healthy Child Development and
Maintaining Strong Parent-Child Bonds," *Pediatrics* 119, no. 1 (2007):
182–191. https://doi.org/10.1542/peds.2006-2697.

124 Elizabeth Prescott, "Foreword to the First Edition," in *The Play's the Thing,* x.

125 L. E. Berk, *Child Development,* 7th ed. (Boston: Allyn & Bacon, 2006).
Cited in *The Play's the Thing,* 4.

126 "Brain Building Through Play," Harvard University Center on the
Developing Child. Accessed August 28, 2024. https://developingchild.
harvard.edu/resources/brainbuildingthroughplay/.

127 *The Play's the Thing,* 4.

128 *The Play's the Thing,* 4.

129 Hirsch-Pasek and Golinkoff, foreword to *The Play's the Thing,* xi-xiii.

130 Early Childhood Australia, *ECA Statement on Play.*

131 Kathy Hirsh-Pasek, "Play + Relationship + Academics: Teaching in the
Ways Kindergartners Learn Best." Webinar hosted by the Campaign for
Grade-Level Reading, August 15, 2023, https://leo.gradelevelreading.net/
event/play-relationship-academics-teaching-in-the-ways-kindergarten-
ers-learn-best/.

132 *The Play's the Thing,* 13.

133 *The Play's the Thing.*

134 Early Childhood Australia, *ECA Statement on Play.*

135 Early Childhood Australia, *ECA Statement on Play.*

136 Early Childhood Australia, *ECA Statement on Play.*

137 Bundy, Anita C. "Play theory and sensory integration." *Sensory integration.
Theory and practice* (1991): 46-68.

138 Kathleen Alfano, "10 Ways Adults Can Be More Playful," *The Genius of
Play.* Accessed August 28, 2024. https://thegeniusofplay.org/genius/
expert-advice/articles/10-ways-adults-can-be-more-playful.aspx#:~:
text=Research%20shows%20that%20being%20playful,%2Dheart%20

and%20free%2Dspirited.

139 *The Play's the Thing.*

140 Nathaniel M. Lambert, Thomas F. Stillman, Joshua A. Hicks, Shanmukh Kamble, Roy F. Baumeister and Frank D. Fincham, "To Belong Is to Matter: Sense of Belonging Enhances Meaning in Life," *Personality and Social Psychology Bulletin* 39, no. 11 (November 2013): 1418–27. https://doi.org/10.1177/0146167213499186.

141 American Psychological Association, "Belonging," *APA Dictionary of Psychology.* Accessed August 28, 2024. https://dictionary.apa.org/belonging.

142 "Belonging," Vocabulary.com. Accessed August 28, 2024. https://www.vocabulary.com/dictionary/belonging.

143 "Belonging," *Cambridge Dictionary.* Accessed August 28, 2024. https://dictionary.cambridge.org/us/dictionary/english/belonging.

144 "Belongingness," Dictionary.com. Accessed August 28, 2024. https://www.dictionary.com/browse/belongingness.

145 Abraham H. Maslow, "A Theory of Human Motivation," *Psychological Review* 50, no. 4 (1943): 370-396. Online version, University of York, accessed August 28, 2024. http://psychclassics.yorku.ca/Maslow/motivation.htm.

146 Brookes Publishing Co., adapted from Denno, Carr and Bell, *Addressing Challenging Behaviors in Early Childhood Settings,* in "15 Things Every Early Childhood Educator Should Do," Brookes Publishing Blog. Accessed August 28, 2024, https://blog.brookespublishing.com/15-things-every-early-childhood-educator-should-do/.

147 Glen Dunlap et al, *Prevent-Teach-Reinforce for Families: A Model of Individualized Positive Behavior Support for Home and Community* (Baltimore, MD: Brookes Publishing Co., 2017). Quote accessed at https://x.com/BrookesPubCo/status/1738186497109442779.

148 "How to Deal with Challenging Behaviors in Preschool," Center for Child Development and Early Learning, November 24, 2022. Accessed August 28, 2024. https://www.cceionline.com/how-to-deal-with-challenging-behaviors-in-preschool/.

149 Harvard University Center on the Developing Child, "What Is Executive Function."

150 Tools of the Mind. Accessed August 28, 2024. https://www.toolsofthemind.org/our-unique-approach.

151 "Brain," *Encyclopædia Britannica,* accessed August 28, 2024, https://www.britannica.com/science/brain.

152 CASEL, "Our History," accessed August 28, 2024, https://casel.org/about-us/our-history/.

153 CASEL, *What Is Social and Emotional Learning?* in *CASEL's Guide to Schoolwide SEL,* accessed August 28, 2024, https://schoolguide.casel.org/what-is-sel/what-is-sel/.

154 Center for Healthy Minds, *Baby Brain and Behavior Project*, accessed August 28, 2024, https://centerhealthyminds.org/science/studies/baby-brain-and-behavior-project.

155 Treves, Hannah, Gregory P. Fricchione, Sarah M. Schnall, and David J. Anderson. *At-Home Use of App-Based Mindfulness for Children: A Randomized Active-Controlled Trial.* Center for Healthy Minds, forthcoming. Accessed August 28, 2024. https://centerhealthyminds.org/assets/files-publications/Treves-et-al-in-press-At-home-use-of-app-based-mindfulness-for-children-A-randomized-active-controlled-trial.pdf.

156 Lisa Flook, "Promoting Prosocial Behavior and Self-Regulatory Skills in Preschool Children Through a Mindfulness-Based Kindness Curriculum," *Developmental Psychology* 51, no. 1 (2015): 44–51, accessed August 28, 2024, https://centerhealthyminds.org/assets/files-publications/FlookPromotingDevPsych.pdf.

157 Center for Healthy Minds, "Understanding Poverty's Impact on the Developing Brain," accessed August 28, 2024, https://centerhealthyminds.org/science/studies/understanding-povertys-impact-on-the-developing-brain.

158 Daniel Goleman, "About," accessed August 28, 2024, https://www.danielgoleman.info/about/.

159 C. Levesque and E.L. Deci, "Intrinsic and Extrinsic Motivation," in *International Encyclopedia of Education*, 3rd ed. (2010), accessed August 28, 2024, https://www.sciencedirect.com/topics/psychology/extrinsic-motivation.

160 Maggie Wooll, MBA, "Extrinsic Motivation: What Is It, and Can It Lead to Fulfillment?" *BetterUp*, updated June 14, 2024, https://www.betterup.com/blog/extrinsic-motivation.

161 UNESCO Institute for Statistics (UIS), "Foundational Skills in the Early Grades," accessed August 28, 2024, https://uis.unesco.org/en/glossary-term/foundational-skills-early-grades.

162 C. Levesque and E.L. Deci, "Intrinsic and Extrinsic Motivation," in *International Encyclopedia of Education*, 3rd ed. (2010), accessed August 28, 2024, https://www.sciencedirect.com/topics/psychology/extrinsic-motivation.

163 Maggie Wooll, MBA, "What Is Intrinsic Motivation? Definition and Examples," *BetterUp*, updated July 24, 2024, https://www.betterup.com/blog/intrinsic-motivation#what-is-intrinsic-motivation.

164 "Knowledge-Based Economy," *IGI Global*, accessed August 28, 2024, https://www.igi-global.com/dictionary/knowledge-based-economy/16497.

165 Sourya Acharya and Samarth Shukla, "Mirror Neurons: Enigma of the Metaphysical Modular Brain," *Journal of Natural Science, Biology, and Medicine* 3, no. 2 (July-December 2012): 118–124. https://doi.

org/10.4103/0976-9668.101878 .

166 A. Arnsten, "Stress Signaling Pathways That Impair Prefrontal Cortex Structure and Function," *Nature Reviews Neuroscience* 10 (June 2009): 410–422. https://doi.org/10.1038/nrn2648.

167 Harvard University Center on the Developing Child, "A Guide to Serve and Return: How Your Interaction with Children Can Build Brains," accessed August 28, 2024, https://developingchild.harvard.edu/ guide/a-guide-to-serve-and-return-how-your-interaction-with-children-can-build-brains/#:~:text=You%20may%20have%20heard%20the,and%20 reach%20their%20full%20potential.

168 CASEL, "What Is Social and Emotional Learning?," *CASEL's Guide to Schoolwide SEL*, accessed August 28, 2024, https://schoolguide.casel. org/what-is-sel/what-is-sel/.

169 Cambridge Dictionary. "Synapse." Accessed August 28, 2024. https:// dictionary.cambridge.org/us/dictionary/english/synapse.

170 Caire, M.J., Reddy, V., and Varacallo, M. "Physiology, Synapse." Updated March 27, 2023. In *StatPearls [Internet]*. Treasure Island, FL: StatPearls Publishing, January 2024-. Available from: https://www.ncbi.nlm.nih. gov/books/NBK526047/#.

www.ingramcontent.com/pod-product-compliance
Lightning Source LLC
Chambersburg PA
CBHW022046020426
42335CB00012B/574